Choosing to Change

It is commonly quoted that the majority of change initiatives fail, and equally common is the reasoning that failure is due to a lack of adequate planning and robust processes to deliver change to the organisation.

However, organisations cannot change; it is only the people in the organisation, and those connected with it, that can change the way they work, think and behave.

Choosing to Change takes an alternative view of the change process, applying thinking from the studies of complexity to explore how change in organisations is driven by individual choice: how the totality of our individual experiences and our aspirations for the future shapes our thinking both consciously and unconsciously, setting out an approach that brings change by choice rather than process.

Through the reflections of those who have experienced change, the book is an exploration of how choice is the basis of all successful change programmes, and how that affects the theory of change management. This book tackles how our future expectations will determine the choices made, and is a vital tool for managers, practitioners and advanced management students.

David Bentley is an independent Change Management Consultant, Visiting Lecturer at the University of Hertfordshire Business School, UK, and Management Trainer. He specialises in leading change, business improvement and leadership development for organisations from global companies to small businesses and charities.

Choosing to Change
An Alternative Understanding of Change Management

David Bentley

LONDON AND NEW YORK

First published 2018
by Routledge
2 Park Square, Milton Park, Abingdon, Oxon OX14 4RN

and by Routledge
711 Third Avenue, New York, NY 10017

Routledge is an imprint of the Taylor & Francis Group, an informa business

© 2018 David Bentley

The right of David Bentley to be identified as author of this work has been asserted by him in accordance with sections 77 and 78 of the Copyright, Designs and Patents Act 1988.

British Library Cataloguing in Publication Data
A catalogue record for this book is available from the British Library

Library of Congress Cataloging in Publication Data
Names: Bentley, David, 1952- author.
Title: Choosing to change : an alternative understanding of change management / David Bentley.
Description: 1 Edition. | New York : Routledge, 2018. | Includes bibliographical references and index.
Identifiers: LCCN 2017036298 (print) | LCCN 2017037783 (ebook) | ISBN 9781315298795 (eBook) | ISBN 9781138237889 (hardback : alk. paper) | ISBN 9781138237896 (pbk. : alk. paper)
Subjects: LCSH: Organizational change. | Leadership. | Strategic planning.
Classification: LCC HD58.8 (ebook) | LCC HD58.8 .B4626 2018 (print) | DDC 658.4/06--dc23
LC record available at https://lccn.loc.gov/2017036298

ISBN: 978-1-138-23788-9 (hbk)
ISBN: 978-1-138-23789-6 (pbk)
ISBN: 978-1-315-29879-5 (ebk)

Typeset in Times New Roman
by Taylor & Francis Books

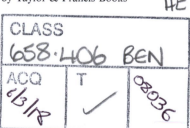

To Jane, Laila and John

Contents

Acknowledgement

The author would like to thank Jim and Ruth for allowing their stories to be told.

Introduction

How often have I said, 'I hate change'? But then, having made a career out of bringing about change in various guises, that may seem a bit of a contradiction. As a young civil engineer in the 1980s I worked on a couple of bypass construction projects that were promoted as 'Turning rail into road'. By constructing the new road along the line of a disused rail track we were improving the local transport network by changing the old for the new. Change in many forms has ironically been a constant in my career.

It is one of the eternal paradoxes of life, that through the ages we constantly seek the security of continuity, sticking to the status quo, whilst life, and the world that we live in, inevitably changes. Politicians and financiers call for stability in the economy, markets and international relations knowing full well that it cannot and does not happen. Harold Macmillan, Britain's prime minister from 1957 to 1963, is reputed to have answered the question put to him by a journalist – 'What is most likely to blow governments off course?' saying 'Events, dear boy, events.' The exact words spoken and indeed the attribution is questioned, but the observation is clear. The best formulated policies and detailed planning will always be victim to the unpredictable – those events that continually emerge creating unexpected change.

Over the course of the past half century I have witnessed a rapid and accelerating pace of change. In technology, the advent of the computer and the revolution in access to information through the internet that has enabled me to research and write this book; in transport, from the postwar spread of the motor car replacing horse drawn transport to the prospect of driverless cars; and in health, evidenced by the extension of life expectancy. In all areas of modern life we are constantly experiencing change, but still we tend to be taken by surprise when it happens and resist it happening.

I have spent my career managing many facets of change. As a construction project manager, I was involved in the planning and creating of change. Whilst it was, on the face of it, the physical change of building roads, utility plants and buildings, it was in fact that most of my time in that role was spent dealing with the unexpected. However detailed the planning and scheduling of the works, a three-dimensional structure is being created from a two-dimensional plan or nowadays perhaps a virtual image. The interpretation of the detail required will always mean that the building created is emergent from those plans and change will be an integral part of the process. The time spent on crafting contracts and resolving disputes arising from the changes that happen are testament to that. Working now in organisational change the same applies. We can plan the change in great detail and strive to make the communication of the change as clear and widespread as possible. We can follow the latest model for change management but the unexpected will always happen. People will react in unpredictable ways, sometimes resisting change that would appear, on the face of it, to be of clear benefit to them, and sometimes changing in ways that they themselves did not expect and being highly successful.

Whilst pursuing my career in change management I have been challenged to radically change my views on the nature of organisations: to re-evaluate what I was doing when planning a construction project and how I understood the reactions of the people I was working with and the cultural changes. By chance I happened to choose to do an MBA course at the University of Hertfordshire that included taking a view of management theory that was developing out of complexity theory – a view that accepts unpredictability, takes human interaction as the basis of organisation and pays attention to what is actually happening rather than creating a model of what we think should be happening. It is in taking this complexity-based view that, I suggest in this book, provides us with an understanding of what motivates people to accept or reject change, providing an approach to managing change that works with individuals to make the choice to change and determines the way that change happens.

The mainstream approach to contemporary management and organisational theory, that has been developed over the course of the twentieth century, is founded on the application of scientific research principles. That is, by conducting experiments, taking measurements and analysing data we can come to a theory of how something works and then use that knowledge to predict what may happen in the future. The ultimate assumption of this way of thinking being that, given sufficient time and research effort, we will eventually discover the 'theory of everything' that will enable us to control our destiny.

If we apply that to organisations, then the theory suggests that by studying how they perform under given conditions, measuring changes in performance and observing behaviour we can understand how they function. We can then develop models of how they should be managed and plan actions for change accordingly. In Chapter 2, we trace how change management practices have developed over the course of the twentieth century on this basis.

At the same time as the dominant theory of management was becoming embedded in organisational thinking, others were approaching the subject from the perspective of social behaviour. In Chapter 3 we will look at, among others, the work of Herbert Mead, the early twentieth-century philosopher, sociologist and psychologist. Mead's philosophy was aligned to the thinking of the school of American Pragmatism: a view that reality is not something that exists independently of the individual but is created by the way in which those individuals act in relation to it. Put simply, an object, such as a chair, only has meaning through the way we interact with it, in this case by sitting on it. So, we construct the reality of our world only by the way that we interact with it. In order to understand the nature of any shared reality, we need to observe what people actually do and how they respond to the world around them. We gain a shared understanding, as we grow up, of what a chair is by observing the way we all use it. The pragmatic approach to understanding is, then, through close contact and immersion in the everyday activities of people and observing how they construct their everyday reality through their interaction with the world around them.

To help us to understand the nature of change in organisations I will be taking an approach based on the principles of pragmatism, using narrative accounts of how people interact with change and how they respond to the challenges presented by change. In this way, we are able to pay attention to what is actually going on in a change situation and to see how it is that people make the choice to change and when they resist. The two narratives, in Chapters 1 and 4 will help us to do that. They tell stories of change from the perspective of those closely involved in the process. They are stories of what actually happened to the people involved, how they experienced the process and how they felt about it, as it happened. As narratives, they are not case studies, that is, idealised accounts detailing a change project from start to finish, but they are verbatim narrative recollections taken from their very individual perspectives.

We start with Jim's story of how he experienced change in his organisation. His story is a very personal account of living though a change process that had a profound effect on his life. Working for the UK arm of a global logistics company as a service depot manager, Jim, and his staff, were taken through a change programme designed to improve efficiency of the operation and develop management skills. His story tells how the process unfolded, the reactions of Jim's staff to the changes and how they made a success of the process. Jim's reflections on his experience and his story of personal development illustrates the role of individual choice in change that forms the theme of this book.

Before we can consider an alternative view of change in organisations we need to understand how the mainstream theories of change management have developed. Chapter 2 recounts the development of mainstream theories of change management from the advent of scientific management theory. By tracing the origins of the current theories of change management we will see how organisations have come to be seen as systems that can be manipulated and redesigned by an external process of management. Rooted in Lewin's (1947) classic three-stage approach to managing change, the treatment of organisations 'as-if' they are systems that can be re-engineered and reset to a new course, has dominated the thinking on change management throughout the twentieth century. With thinking on leadership reflecting this same view, change is considered to be a top-down driven process that can be project managed through clear visions, communication and careful planning. Jim's story in Chapter 1 puts this approach in the context of a live organisation and we can see the extent to which this view of change management chimes with Jim's experience and where more complex issues are at play.

In forming an alternative view of change management, in Chapter 3, we start with the organisation 'as-is', that is, as a group of interacting individuals sharing a common goal of delivering a product or service. Through the study of non-linear networks, we can form an understanding of how changing patterns of behaviour emerge from the interaction of individuals in that organisation. The development of complexity theory, coupled with social psychology and modern neuroscience, provides us with an alternative way of understanding the change process.

It is the unconscious reality that we construct from birth that drives our behaviour in the present. It is the key to how we interact with each other in our organisations and in life generally. Our unconscious reality drives our expectation of the future and determines how we react to the prospect of change. The ongoing pattern of change is the emergent and unpredictable process arising from that interaction. In taking this view, we can pay attention to what is actually happening and start to work with that in the change process.

Ruth's story, in Chapter 4, is one of a learning process and the development of an understanding of change. Circumstances conspired to put Ruth into the position of managing director of an established packing and freighting company that was facing an industry-wide process of modernisation and globalisation. Having joined the company initially just to 'help out' and without formal training in managing change, she formed a practical understanding of the subject by dealing with it at the sharp end. Working nowadays as an independent business consultant and business school lecturer, her approach recognises that change is driven, not by the visions of senior management but by the choices made by individuals.

The study of non-linear networks shows how they create novel patterns of behaviour as the connectivity increases, that is, the degree to which each individual is able to influence the behaviour of those connecting to it. This is seen in nature, in phenomena such as the flocking of birds and, in the longer term, the evolution of species. We can recognise this in human behaviour and, in Chapter 5, we carry this understanding forward to consider how organisations use these emerging patterns to improve their competitiveness. It is also this increasing connectivity, leading to trust and belief in an ability to face change, that allows us to take a step into the unknown, with the confidence to embrace change and trust in an emerging solution.

The forming, and constant reforming, of our personal realities is fundamental to the way we interact with each other and how change emerges from that. In Chapter 6 we look at how we communicate with each other and the power of storytelling and narrative learning in forming the realities that drive communication in all its forms. We see, in the stories of change from Jim and

Ruth, the power of the developing narrative in influencing the choices made to adopt or reject the changes. The ability to have open and challenging conversations that communicate with, and help us to constantly reform, our unconscious reality is the key that enables us to make the choice to change.

Bringing all of these ideas together in Chapter 7, we consider what it means to take this alternative approach to managing change, an approach that puts individual choice ahead of a managed process.

Using a complexity understanding of what is actually happening with individuals interacting in organisations and the unpredictable and emergent nature of change, we put individual choice at the centre of change management. It is the unconscious reality that drives choice, and by making that explicit we can influence the narrative shared in the organisation to promote the emergence of positive change. We address the question of what it means to have challenging conversations and to employ narrative learning in organisations, enabling groups to move to a position of creativity, and to the point where they can embrace the emergent and unpredictable nature of change and make the choice to change with confidence.

Reference

Lewin, K., 1947. Frontiers in Group Dynamics: Concepts, Method and Reality in Social Science; Social Equilibria and Social Change. *Human Relations* 1: 5–41.

1 Experiencing change
The depot manager's story

We start our exploration of change with a story of experiencing change: an account of a successful change programme seen from the perspective of a key manager in the company undergoing the process.

Jim is the manager of a vehicle service depot for a large UK logistics company which had, in the previous few years, been taken over by a European operator and was about to undergo a change programme designed to improve efficiency, quality and manager competence.

This is Jim's story.

Past changes

"My real passion in life has always been sport and particularly football. I played semi-professionally but never quite made it into the top flight, so, I then took it up as a coach. The highlight of that was spending seven years working abroad as a professional coach. One of my claims to fame was that two of my protégés made it into their national team. When we returned to the UK I felt that my pursuit of a career where I could be doing what I really wanted to was over. Through a friend, I got a job as a customer service assistant with a logistics company. I settled into that and worked my way up to be the depot manager at their Southeast location about an hour's drive from my home on the South Coast.

"After a couple of years in that post the company was taken over by a European operator and we went through a major change from working for an English firm to a pan-European company. Our processes completely changed. We changed the way we did things. How we did health and safety and different work practices. We accepted the changes quite well. We met with our staff, that is, I met with the staff, to let them know what was going on.

"I would like to think that the positive attitude was a lot down to me. Probably my being a bit older, a bit wiser, and having worked abroad for an overseas company, I knew it wasn't going to change. The new company wasn't going to turn around and say 'Oh let's just do it their old way' because they had just bought us. So, it was important to get across to the staff, that it's not going to change. That we need to be positive. If we are negative nothing is going to happen to change things.

"So just purely by, I suppose it was just a case of putting my arm around people and saying: 'you know it's going to be alright, there's a light at the end of the tunnel'. I think it was just forward thinking that this is the way it is going to be. Let's grab it with both hands. Go on the road, as they say. So, we were one of the ones that were recognised where there was a good attitude and we just moved forward."

Beginning the change

"Again, a couple of years passed as things settled down before we heard that the UK board of the company had decided to bring in consultants to look into the way we do everything. They wanted to review all the processes, look at best practice and make changes to improve the efficiency and quality of vehicle servicing.

"We were in the second phase and the feeling at the start was:

'What do they know?'

'Why do they want to do this?'

'We're fine': all the usual things that staff talk about.

'We don't need anybody else to tell us what to do. We know, we have been doing it for twenty years.'

"Those were the initial responses we had.

"The only thing that I would say, I had a little bit of doubt about, was the communication. We just got to hear that they were trialling some new processes. The consultants were in four of the depots around the country looking at our processes and the way that we do everything. So, the people weren't really getting anything specific. They didn't say 'this is what we are going to do, we are going to do this or we are going to do that. We just knew that 'the consultants were coming around and you will deal with them'.

"My workshop supervisor and I got the chance to go to our Southwest Depot and meet some of the consultants who were trialling the processes there but that did not go well. He was very anti the consultants, saying:

'What does this bloke know?'. 'I've been doing this for thirty-five years and he's been here five minutes.'

"So, that was typical of the initial reactions.

"Given our success in going through the changes when we were taken over I was quite positive. I don't mind things changing if I feel it's for the better. The worry I had was that certain members of staff were being quite anti. Uncertain about what the consultants are going to do and how they were going to do it, so they were apprehensive about the future.

"They were more worried about, not their jobs, but someone telling them how to do something that they thought they were doing right anyway. So, they were raising all sorts of questions. You know, 'well what about this, what about that?' They, I think, went straight on to the defensive before anything happened.

"So again, as I did with the takeover, I held a staff meeting. But because we didn't really know, I couldn't explain or say 'this is what is going to happen'. The only thing I could say, as I said before was 'we should be positive, it's not going to change'. They're not going to say 'no' to the consultants, 'don't bother to go to the Southeast Depot'. So, in the workshop, the troops were not happy. In the office, the staff, they were fifty-fifty but they didn't really know what it was going to be like."

The change programme

"The Board, together with the consultants, had put together a communication pack which addressed the reasons for the programme and showed some of the new best practice processes that they had identified in operation in their continental depots. It included a message from the UK managing director, intended to reassure the staff that the programme was not intended as a criticism of the current staff and procedures but a process to make things even better.

"The four depots that were doing the trials got the message at the start of that period and then the other depot managers got it through the operations managers letting us know what was going on. There was going to be a conference call for those four depots and I saw some of the slides that were part of the communications pack at that time. Looking back on it now, I think it was alright and I thought, at the time, that it would be good for the depot. I didn't realise then, however, how good it would be for me personally.

"The change programme was set to roll out in my depot over a twelve-week period. Starting with a two-day training course and then followed by a sequence of process roll-out, coaching and personnel development. During this period, my depot would be supported by one of the consultants visiting one to two days per week to coach the staff and introduce the new processes and working practices, monitor progress and work with individual staff members to help them through the change.

"The programme was implemented across groups of four depots at a time and we were in the first phase after the four trial depots. We started with the training sessions. I didn't, personally, think that the training really explained what was going to happen in the depot. I did the training and went away with the thought of it's a good idea but I couldn't work it out in my own mind, how it was going to work in the depots. We went through all the slides, like staff management, measuring technician efficiency, health and safety and how to do one-to-one meetings. But I couldn't work out in my mind, when I left and got in the car, how it was going to be. Two others from my depot, the workshop supervisor and the planner, also went on the training and they both came back saying things like, 'I don't understand it.' Particularly from the supervisor saying, 'It's a load of rubbish.'

"There was quite a bit of negative feedback and that made me a bit nervous. I think it was just that it was going be outsiders who were going into their domain. They were worried that someone was going to come in and say to them:

'You're doing this wrong, you're doing that wrong, you need to do this, do that.'

"They were thinking: 'Why should we change things that we have been doing for twenty-five years?' I heard the expression, 'If it is not broken why are we fixing it?'

"So, there was a lot of uncertainty about what was going to happen. They weren't being specific about things that they were concerned about, it was just a feeling:

'Why are they doing this, why are they spending a fortune doing this?'

'Who are these people?'

'What do they know about trucks?'

"There wasn't any certainty about what we were going to do, like, this is how we are going to measure our efficiency and this is why we are going to record it. There was more a sense of being told you are just going to change! So, there was, I think, a lot of anti-feeling in certain parts.

"Personally, I could see, that is part of me could see, it was going to be good but I couldn't see it working in the depot. I went away just thinking, how are we going to do this? How will it be beneficial? How will I explain this to the staff? Saying 'it will be really good' when in my own mind, I wasn't sure how it would go. I didn't feel that I was going to be the barrier but I just wasn't sure about it."

Implementing the change

"In the week following the training courses we started to implement the processes. The consultant came to the depot for his first day with us in the middle of that week. That is when things began to fall into place at least as far as the new processes and working practices were concerned. He explained to us what was going to happen, how it would evolve over the three months that he would be around. Above all he was just bringing lots of stuff for us to do.

"To start with, I think, it was again the same problem, there was much apprehension about what was going to happen and what the real motive of the consultant was. We hadn't spoken yet to the staff so they were still uncertain. This consultant turns up and was watching what they were doing and again there was some negative attitude from the senior people where they were saying 'I know what I am doing.' But once we had sat down and spoken about it and sorted out what we were going to do, what the process was and how long it was going to be, then I could see where we were going. I could see what we were going to do and I was a little bit more confident.

"On the first day, he observed the staff, initially it was just to see what their job roles were. Explaining to them what we were going to do. What meetings we were going to have and so it was just laying the ground rules for what we were going to do going forward for the twelve weeks. We were introduced to doing the conference calls, which is something some of them had never done before, so people were apprehensive about doing that. So, on the first day we set the ground rules, we basically had a chat. After he left I had a staff meeting and tried to reassure the staff that I thought there would be a good outcome to the programme. Again, I was saying that it was a positive thing, 'we are going to have a few bumps in the road, as we know but it will be positive for us'. If the staff were positive as well it would be alright. Still lots of people were not so sure about what we were going to do.

"The way I finished it was, 'well we've done it once before, and we came out of it the other side, we can do it again. We have got to be open to what people tell us, even if it is bad we've got to be open, we are all here to discuss it'.

"Personally, I thought it would be good not only for the depot but for me as a manager. I felt it's a good tool for me to make me a better manager and I was quite positive with it from the start. I wasn't really a negative thinker, you know, but once I had a better understanding, I thought it would be a good thing.

"Over the week following the first day, with the consultant the feedback was:

'I don't know if I trust him.'

'What's he doing?'

'Why is he watching me?'

'Why can't he watch someone else?'

"It was just so very guarded.

'He knows nothing about trucks, so what is he going to tell me about trucks?'

'What do they know?'

"The people who had been doing it for years and years were just very cautious, they didn't think it would work.

"Then, at the start of the second week we were involved in our first conference call. At that early stage, we were not contributing any data from my depot. There were a lot of slides but we were only listening in at that stage. We were just looking at what the other depots were doing and I said to my people that were listening 'there is nothing difficult here'. But again, they were still saying:

'Oh, I'm not sure about this. I don't like this. It's more work. I work hard enough as it is. If you want me to do this as well it's extra.'

"As we moved forward over the coming weeks, we were talking to the staff, we were doing one-to-one sessions and we were doing formal observations. For the first couple of weeks of doing the observations there was still a lot of 'What are you watching me for?' But as we progressed it changed to 'Oh aren't you doing my observation?' as they got involved and began to see the results of that for the depot reported in the conference calls.

"In the office, it was quicker because they wanted to see what score they were going to get. 'Did I do this? Did I do that?' I think what it did was, it enabled me to start recognising what my staff were doing and what they weren't doing. So, it was, for me, a good tool and we could move forward."

The Values and Beliefs sessions

"In the third week, we started the one-to-one process with the Values and Beliefs sessions and that was the point where things really started to change. Overall, we started to move forward as a depot, we had a few setbacks along the way, but these sessions really made the difference. For me, after that I never looked back from that point.

"Using two sets of cards prepared with values written on one set and beliefs on the other I was asked, by the consultant, to identify the five values and five beliefs about myself that I held most important. Picking the values that are most important to me was relatively easy and I don't think that they were much different to those that most people would pick. However, when it came to my strongly held beliefs about myself it was very different. One of the cards stood out from all the rest in the early ones that came out and as we worked through the rest of them, eliminating those that meant less, that one stayed at the top. That card simply said, 'I'm not tall enough.'

"The conversation that flowed from that was at the same time both difficult and a revelation for me. It was the first time that I had sat down to say things like that. When I was young my Mum took me to the hospital, I wasn't growing properly and I had a problem with growth and everything. I was the youngest of four boys and being small I wouldn't be in the football team and even if I was picked I wasn't big enough. As a professional footballer, I never quite made it into the top flight and I always had in the back of my mind the reason was that I was not good enough because of my lack of height. The other beliefs about myself that I picked out just served to reinforce my lack of self-esteem that was wrapped up in the belief that my lack of height had and was continuing to hold me back in being successful.

"As the conversation opened out into some of the issues I was experiencing in my work life, such as finding it difficult to delegate work or manage my long working days, I began to see things more clearly. Yes, I think it was the values and beliefs that brought it home to me that although I am only five foot six inches tall it doesn't matter. Nowadays, I don't think that I am small anymore. I think that this was quite a big thing to get over. I walk tall now. That was quite a difficult thing to do but I'm glad I have done it. Whilst I was nervous before it, I didn't know before what was going to come of it. As we were doing it, as it was explained to me, I actually walked out of it thinking, 'I've changed, I'm going to change, I'm a different person now.' I was, like, 'I'm not small in stature, I'm a leader, a manager,' and I think from that day it changed me in what I did and how I did it. I was more confident in how I did it.

"My values and beliefs session was the first of the set that were done at the depot with the key staff. Having been through the process I was able to reassure those who followed me that it was nothing to be worried about and that

I had found it to be a very positive experience. The sessions were held in confidence, so I don't know exactly what came out of the sessions with the other staff members but I can say that they became more confident. I don't know if they bought into it fully, as I did, because they are still behaving in the way they did. But they are more confident in the way they are doing their jobs.

"The Values and Beliefs session enabled me to reflect on the way I behaved as a manager. I was doing everything. I admit, quite feely now, I did everything but did nothing. I just, as it were, forwarded everything to myself, thinking 'I'll do this, I'll do that.' My lack of confidence in myself, my underlying assumption that 'I was not good enough to succeed', was preventing me in having confidence in my staff. My reaction then was to do everything myself. Obviously, looking back, the knock-on from that was they were under-utilised and dissatisfied.

"Building on the Values and Beliefs session the consultant challenged me to make a difference in the way I managed my workload. I took on improving the way I managed my time. By keeping a detailed diary of what I was actually doing I was able to identify those activities that needed my input, where I could add value, and those that could be done perfectly well by others. I looked at how I was delegating, or not, to my staff using the learning from the training session. I started explaining what I wanted them to do. I started to give people jobs to do that did not need my input and that was good for me. It made me a different person, a different manager. I went from being someone that, well, I could always leave what I was doing at the gate when I drove out of the depot without taking it home with me. But now I was more comfortable with what I was doing and it being a part of my life. I could now give people things to do, so I had the time to concentrate on things that were happening. I had the feeling, like, 'This is so different.'

"It wasn't, though, all plain sailing from that point on. I lost two members of staff within three weeks of the programme starting. The workshop supervisor was very unhappy with what he was being asked to do. He didn't want to get involved with it and thought it was a stupid process. I tried to have a conversation with him to persuade him to see it through but to no avail. I thought at the time 'How are we going to survive, what are we going to do?' He had been with us a long time. So, yeah, it was rough. It was the same with the service representative. She had been with us three years. She did the same thing, wanting to know 'Why are you watching me? Why are we doing this? I'm good at my job! I know what I'm doing!' So we had the same conversation but she was not to be persuaded. In the end though we survived and I think were better for it.

"So, not for all of us, but for me personally with what I went through then I see not only the change in myself but in some of them as well. They started to get more confident about what they were doing, actually doing more work. They'll be sitting in on conference calls and being proud of what we are doing, and then they never looked back, they were all for it."

Instigating one-to-one sessions

"The outcome from the Values and Beliefs sessions set action plans for development over the remaining period of the programme and then, as that came to an end, for the future. These plans were monitored, discussed and built through more formal one-to-one sessions at regular intervals and informal chats and coaching at each visit. The one-to-ones were also extended across all the staff and technicians. I was quite nervous about doing the one-to-one meetings with the staff, particularly as I was being observed and critiqued by the consultant as well. I wanted to do my best by each member of staff and let them reap the benefits that I was getting from the programme. I wanted to improve my skills at the same time but being under scrutiny while you are doing it is never easy. Added to that I've worked with these people all this time. We used to have a personal development review once a year which was a bit of a tick-box, not a tick-box exercise, but a tick-box form. It was a sort of 'Oh you did that well, what do you think?' conversation but we never really asked them what they wanted.

"What did they want to get out of working?

"How do they want to progress?

"Then, all of a sudden, I'm presented with this form and I'm talking to my staff. Talking about what they have done well and thanking them for doing a good job. Actually, they responded and they came back saying:

'I think I've done well this week.'

'I would like to improve how I do this.'

"In this way, we were changing the whole structure of how we were doing one-to-ones.

"So, the first one-to-one I did with the customer service manager, who has been there for fifteen years, I was really quite apprehensive about it but it turned out to be one of the best jobs I've ever done. Just by purely talking to him, taking an interest about what he wanted to do. Talking about the different things that he could get to do that he hadn't done in all of those fifteen years. All of a sudden, we were developing our own staff. I saw that, through the first one, and for a manager, for me, it was the tool to use. I was able to repeat that with my other direct reports and we coached them to cascade the meeting down so that all members of staff benefitted and were able to progress. As that unfolded over the weeks, particularly after the initial rounds where people were getting over their fears about the process, things really started to improve. By this time, we were absolutely flying.

"We were reviewing our progress against the other depots, in the weekly conference calls, and getting good results. The negative stuff just wasn't there anymore. Well obviously, the technicians, being technicians, were still asking 'Why are they making us do this?' But as soon as we started saying, 'well we are at 80 per cent efficiency or we were at 85 per cent and we are in the green on the charts and we could see progress on the change curve. It was the feel-good factor that was doing us all good. It was, like, everybody had bought into it and it was just a happy place to work.

"Through the one-to-ones, I was able to explain how the efficiency measures that we had put in place were working and how we could use the data that we were collecting to further improve things. How we could look at eliminating wasted time and effort and work together to improve skills and the quality of the work. We published the data on how we had all used our time each week and discussed it at the daily meetings as well.

"There came to be a friendly competitive spirit amongst the staff and particularly the technicians. They came to see in the weekly results and the teleconferences how they were doing in comparison with the other depots on the programme. A fact that spurred them on, not wanting to be the ones held to account on the call.

"We are still doing the quality checks that we started with the programme: we do five per week per technician. They still all want to know their scores. I think the good thing about the quality checks and the discussion about them, that we have in the one-to-ones is that, if we do find something, then the technician is now quite happy to listen and say 'Oh OK, I did miss that.' Whereas before when we did that, at the start, it was like 'No it was perfect, what about this, what about that?' I think now they are quite happy and they want to know if they have done something wrong or what you find.

"I think that it was through the one-to-ones that the change with the quality checks came about. I set targets in the one-to-ones, once we had got some consistency with the scores. If they were scoring ninety, I would say I want ninety-two or ninety-three. So, that mindset of, you know, checking properly, picking each other up when things were not up to standard, that still goes on. I think, in the end, the one-to-ones are a way to speak to people, to explain what we are doing, ask them if they are having problems or is there a training issue that they need help with? It's quite a civilised conversation."

My personal change

"Through all of this, the Values and Beliefs, carrying out the one-to-ones, the observations and the communication meetings, I've changed, I'm a much more confident character. I manage people better now. I manage myself better now. I structure my day a lot better now and I've just gone from strength to strength. Since that time, I've been promoted twice. I'm now in a roving troubleshooting role. So, it has totally changed me. When we first started, I wanted to do everything myself and cared about everything, that is I took care of everything. I still care about the staff but I cared, then, about what they would say. Now I trust my staff to do what they do. I can delegate work to them with confidence.

"I think they see me differently now as well, which is great. It's good because they think I've progressed. I never thought I'd say it, in my lifetime, but I'm quite ambitious now. I think they know I want to do something else.

They know I'm done now and that they now have a good depot with a good reputation. They know it's time for me to move on.

"As I said, I lived in the States for seven years as a professional football coach and I felt that, after that, the work I was doing would never be as good again. Now, in the last year I actually like going to work. I love what I do. It's maybe not the best job in the world but I really enjoy working now and I made it pretty clear once we had gone through the programme that I didn't want to stay sitting in just one depot. I was quite vocal in my desire to do something else. Through the programme I ended up helping at the West London, South Wales, South Midlands and East London depots. So, I now do what I want to do. Before the change I just drove to the depot, did my stuff and drove home again but now I'm involved with the others I love what I do. I think I have become much more of a people person now.

"A big part of it now is that I am enjoying the challenge. When I went to the West London depot it was still quite negative. Although they had been through the same programme with the same people – so why was it quite different there?

"I went there initially just to watch and observe, look and see what they were doing, and how they were doing it. To see why it was things had not worked so well there. I found that they were very anti. They didn't like the programme, saying that 'All of it's rubbish,' and very much on a downer.

"So, I started going there three days a week just to observe what they were doing. I was then tasked with trying to help them gain the benefit from the pro-gramme that we had achieved at my depot. So, through my own experience in the programme, and my new-found confidence, I found I could actually sit with both the managers there and have a quite open and frank discussion about what they were doing and what they were going to do. I was able to tell them, as I did with my staff that, 'You need to do this. It's not negative, it's a positive.' To start with they were saying 'It's not like the Southeast Depot here,' and I'm saying 'Yes, it is, it's just that you are about six weeks behind them.' Having explained things to the people there, we started to change things like the way that we did the yard and the way we did the observations. One of the managers left and the supervisor, whose struggle with his role had been highlighted by the programme, was moved to a lead hand position. So now, through their hard work and the advances we have made, it's one of the company's better locations.

"Some of the people at that depot had struggled with the Values and Beliefs sessions. They had not taken on board the issues raised in their own sessions, as they affected their work and their willingness to change as I had. There was some resentment at the issues being brought out and they had reacted negatively to the experience. I don't think that, perhaps, everyone is as confident about what they want to do.

"The one person who is coming out of it best now, though, is, or was then, the customer service manager. Because he has now been promoted to depot manager. He is actually a much better manager now than he was previously.

We have continued the one-to-ones and I think some of the issues raised by the values and beliefs have been addressed by him. He is much more positive now. He is much more confident. Previously, he didn't want to go anywhere and didn't want to say anything. Now he goes to conferences and is quite happy to seek out clients to talk to. He is now a changed person. I would say that he has changed by having things explained, just in a different way to the way he's tried it before.

"I think a good example was when I explained to him how we needed a yard person, and how we had benefitted from that in the Southeast. He was, like, 'Well I tried to do that but no one wants to do it.' I said to him 'Have you asked them?' There was no answer to that! So, I asked them. Now we have a good yard person who's making a big difference and he doesn't want to come off it. I think the difference was that it was coming from somebody within the company rather than external. I do think that you have to follow through on it properly with your own people. Because I feel that the staff will open up more to a company person, if you like. One perhaps on the same level. I think that when you have the consultants come in and set out what was going to happen then it is not always in everybody's comfort zone. There was quite a bit of that at that depot."

Leadership

"I do think that senior management has quite an effect on the success of a programme like that. For us they were generally positive about it but I don't know if they all were. I sit here now and think, having listened to the conference calls and being on the operations manager's calls, I don't know if they all bought it. A bit like the staff in the depot. I think some of them did and some didn't. There were all the messages like, 'It's going to be good for us,' but I think I'm not sure that they all believed all of it. I think that the MD was right behind it but a few others I'm less sure about.

"I was quite lucky in my operations manager. He was very positive right from the start and I was able to progress quite quickly in the programme. When my manager was away I was invited into the operations manager's conference call. So, I listened to senior managers on the calls going through the process, talking about the programme. That's where I got the feeling that not everybody bought it. But, yes, he was really good and still is. He loves the programme and talks about it all the time. So, he believes in it and bought into it fully and he has the best area in the country. All his managers have progressed within the two years that we have been doing it. He was positive and his manager, in turn, was too, so he had good backing and it trickles down. He was fully involved both with the programme and its implementation at the depot level. He did the one-to-ones for his reports. He was involved in and did the observations and quality checks. He was always coming to the depot, talking to people.

"One thing that the West London Depot didn't have was a positive operations manager. Tellingly, some of the people that didn't like it, were not positive about it, are not here anymore. There are some people that struggled with it because I think they're not sure of themselves but we still have the processes in place and now we are starting to fine tune them and they are beginning to work."

Reflecting on the changes

"The real turning point for me was the Values and Beliefs and the work we did with the diaries, where it's all written down. It seems very simple now but that really was the point where it all changed for me. That's the story I tell about the programme, for me personally. I bring it up quite a lot. I bring it up at all the depots that I go to where I do the same sort of thing. I did it with the people here, saying, 'How do you structure your day? How does your day go?' I keep the notes I have from that point in my briefcase. I happened to look at them the other day, I thought how much I have changed. My wife has noticed a big change in me as well. I think she's thinking, I'm happier. She said to me the other day that I keep saying '… when I get promoted'. But she points out that, 'You said five years ago, "If I maybe make depot manager, that's me done." Now you want to be an operations manager, you are a "trouble shooter for the company", now you are not at home' – that's how I've changed. Now I'm better at communicating and I can help people make their own way I think I make a difference. Being able to do this sort of thing now. This is what I want to do. You see, people are different. It's not just about explaining processes. It's about how you change your own mind. Just talking to people, saying 'Try this,' talking to them.

"The company sometimes like to do the disciplinary. No! Let's just talk to people. Let's have that conversation. 'Have they got a problem? Have you asked them?' It's just all that sort of thing now. So, having more confidence about that has made me a better person. Made me a better manager. My operations director said to me 'You have changed from a manager to a really good manager.' Then he turned around to the managing director and said 'He's a really good manager now.' He knows the change in me."

Thoughts on Jim's story

The change process that Jim experienced followed what I would describe as the 'conventional' thinking on how such a programme should be managed. The required changes in the ways of working were determined through an assessment exercise designed to identify best practice in the industry. The assessment was carried out by the senior managers working with the consultant and the identified changes packaged for implementation. A communication plan was put in place and followed with mixed effectiveness, as Jim has observed, and following an introductory training phase the implementation programme was rolled out by the consultants. This is a conventional view of change, where it is seen as something that is done to others or, for those on the receiving end, that is done to them. A view reflected by the language of management and implementation.

As Jim recounts, a number of key performance measures were put in place to track the outcome of the process and generally these showed improvements in performance over the implementation period. So, in practical terms this example would not be counted among the vast majority of change programmes that fail when measured in this way.

Jim's story of the change tells of the casualties that occurred as a result of the choices some of the members of staff made. For those people, the requirement to change was more than they could accept. This was something that was repeated across the business as the programme was rolled out. By contrast, the change in Jim's performance and his move beyond his base depot to a roving troubleshooting role was one of the success stories. The change in Jim's approach to his role and his life was not explicit in the original plan. It was not one of the things that could be measured and reported on. Jim made a choice to change his reality, the way he felt about himself. His progress and developing role was unplanned and solely emergent from the process.

However carefully a change programme is designed, planned, communicated and rolled out, these are the sort of unpredictable outcomes that we see: outcomes that emerge entirely from the individual choices that are made as the present unfolds. It is from this individual perspective that we will explore the nature of change and set out an alternative view of change management in this volume. First though, we will establish how the thinking behind the 'conventional' change management process has evolved over the past hundred years.

2 The managed approach to change

The management view of the change process

Scientific management

Frederick Winslow Taylor was an obsessive. Obsessive about the pursuit of efficiency both in his working and his personal life. In the early years of the twentieth century the growth of industry, from the revolution in manufacturing of the previous century, matured into a quest for efficiency to boost profits. Taylor's obsession matured into the opportunity to change business thinking.

In 1878 Taylor joined the Midvale Steel Company in Philadelphia as a machine shop labourer, and the direction for management thought across the coming century was set. The son of Franklin Taylor, a wealthy Princeton educated lawyer, and Annette Taylor (née Winslow), an ardent abolitionist and direct descendant of a Mayflower emigrant, he was expected to take up law. However, his promising academic career, that culminated in passing the entrance exam for Harvard, was cut short by deteriorating eyesight from his nocturnal studies. This though turned to Frederick's favour as his eyesight recovered with the ending of long hours of study and he was able to take an apprenticeship as a patternmaker at the Enterprise Hydraulic Works in 1875. His move to the Midvale Steel Company took him from labourer through the ranks to chief engineer, and his passion for data and work efficiency took him to global recognition and the founding of the management science now known as Taylorism or Scientific Management.

In 1881, aged 25, Taylor introduced to the steel plant the idea of time study (later to become known as time and motion study). He passionately believed that the efficiency of any activity could be increased and the energy required to complete it reduced by observation and the elimination of waste. This passion extended to his own recreational pursuit of walking in the countryside, where he measured his progress and sought to cover the distance with the greatest efficiency and with the minimum of energy in crossing the obstacles in his path.

Taylor returned to studying and completed a degree in mechanical engineering at the Stevens Institute of Technology in 1883. In 1890 he joined the Manufacturing Investment Company where he established a 'new profession' of Consulting Engineer in Management – the forerunner of today's management consultant. Retiring from industry at the age of 45, Taylor devoted the rest of his working life to the development of his theories of scientific management, publishing many influential papers. His *Principles of Scientific Management* was published in 1911 and set the parameters for the development of management theory.

Taylor's primary focus was the efficient performance of individual tasks within a wider production activity such as the shovelling of coal into a furnace in the making of steel. He believed that applying a scientific approach, i.e. the observation of the performance of the task and the collection and analysis of the data related to that task, would identify the most efficient way to complete it. This approach applied to all the tasks involved in the overall activity would then lead to the maximum benefit of both employer and employee. The employer would gain the maximum production and therefore revenue from those that he employed. The employee would earn more from his share of the savings made in employing less people. In the relatively buoyant steel production of the time Taylor did not see any difficulty in shedding labour from one task as there was always a demand for additional labour through the expansion earned from greater efficiency. His views were not universally shared by the workers, who saw them as a direct threat to their job security. Taylor, however, maintained his pursuit of the one best, most efficient, way that he believed was there to be discovered for any industrial activity.

Whilst Taylor believed that the benefit of his scientific management in improving efficiency was self-evident and would therefore be embraced by employers and employees alike, he was also concerned with how those who did not share his views might be managed to adopt improved methods. He acknowledged that those paid on an hourly rate would not necessarily benefit monetarily from increasing their output. Those who felt that their jobs were threatened by the changes would be inclined to resist them. On these issues Taylor believed in the importance of education and training of both the employers and employees to understand the benefits of scientific management and how, given that there would always be periods of lesser prosperity, in the long term all would be better off. Frederick Taylor's focus in scientific management on observation, data analysis and the introduction of new working methods set the framework of change management for the future. Issues such as the resistance to change, the need to communicate the benefits of the new way and an understanding of the need to change remain, in the twenty-first century, the principle concerns of professional change managers.

Taylor's approach followed the established scientific principle of reducing activities to their component tasks. By analysing and improving each of the separate components the efficiency of the overall activity is optimised. In this way, the one best way can be defined and maximum efficiency achieved. This is what Taylor referred to as the substitution of science for the rule of thumb (Taylor, 1911).

It is a part of human nature to seek to control the things that affect one's life; to reduce uncertainty and order events to one's advantage. Whilst we all know instinctively that the future cannot be predicted or confidently shaped to our will, we still seek to do so. Ever since men and women first gained the ability to think about their situation and consider how their existence is determined by factors outside their understanding, they have sought to gain influence and control. From the earliest forms of ritual sacrifice, to please the Gods, to modern attempts to manage the environment, humans have striven to reduce the uncertainty of their existence. The promise of scientific endeavour down the centuries has been that if we just understand more, by delving ever deeper into the minutiae of the physical world, it would ultimately lead to the theory of everything and the ability to control our world. Ironically, the deeper we delve the more we unearth the complex nature of our world and its unpredictable nature. We understand instinctively that we cannot control our destiny but we continue to believe that we can. We assume the recognised philosophical device of thinking 'as-if' that were true.

It was Immanuel Kant, the eighteenth-century German philosopher, who described the tendency to act 'as-if' something is true where in fact a rational, or perhaps more in-depth, assessment of the facts would say that it was not true. Kant focused on the philosophical arguments surrounding religious belief, but we can also see it in more contemporary and, perhaps simpler examples. Newton's laws of motion are generally accepted and widely used in mechanics, but they make one fundamental assumption in ignoring the effect of friction between surfaces in contact. This greatly simplifies things and in effect makes the calculations solvable. Clearly you cannot say, rationally, that friction does not have an effect but we choose, in accepting these laws, to act 'as-if' it was true. Similarly, in the world of structural analysis, where we are designing perhaps bridges or buildings, it is assumed for simplicity that all materials have uniform characteristics. They each have the same defined strength and degree of flexibility under load such that we can calculate how much material is needed to construct whatever we are designing. However, as any designer will tell you, materials are never completely uniform in their characteristics and it is just not possible to know exactly how they will perform when incorporated into a structure. We then render the unknowable into a predictable, and therefore calculable, state by acting 'as-if' it is uniform. In this particular case, having completed our detailed calculations of the materials needed we add a generous safety factor to account for the unknown. As Hans Vaihinger puts it in his work, *Philosophy of 'As-If'*, we willingly accept falsehoods or fictions in order to live peacefully in an irrational world (Vaihinger, 1911).

Systems thinking

Working from this scientific background, Ludwig von Bertalanffy, in the mid-twentieth century, formulated the General Systems Theory. Born at the turn of the century near Vienna, in Austria, Bertalanffy's life spanned three quarters of the century and great advances in scientific understanding. Having gained a

Ph.D. in biology he became a professor at the University of Vienna and sub-sequently in London, Montreal, Ottawa, California, Alberta and finally New York. He died in 1972. His work studying systems and in developing his general theory extended beyond biology to inform thought in the areas, among many, of cybernetics, philosophy and sociology. Bertalanffy's work, contrary to the reductionist approach of general science, studied the inter-relationships between component parts of a system, such as a biological organism or an organisation, and how those parts form the whole. He concluded that the classical science, and in particular the second law of thermodynamics, that governs the behaviour of closed systems models was not adequate for understanding open systems which are subject to change from their external environment. That is, the behaviour of open systems, such as organisations, that are continually affected by external influences, such as market forces and changing technology, is not determinate. So, therefore, they do not operate like machines. The outcome of their activities is not fully predictable or indeed understandable. However, the study of the component parts and their relationships does imply that they may be understood as a closed system if we could only understand fully and manage those relationships. So, from a general systems theory point of view, organisations can be treated 'as-if' they are rationally behaving systems.

Peter Senge in his book on what he terms 'the learning organisation' (Senge, 1990), uses the analogy of the organisation 'as-if' it was a system. He treats the individuals (or component parts) and their relationships as a whole, one that is endowed with the ability to learn and react to its changing cir-cumstances to be successful. The assumption of a 'systems-like' behaviour is reflected in the language of organisations, for example 'leverage', providing 'feedback' and 'oiling the wheels' of industry.

Lewin's change process

In 1947 Kurt Lewin published his work on social change (Lewin, 1947) that set the pattern for change management that is still in common use today. Lewin was born in September 1890 in Mogilno in what is now Poland. The son of a general store keeper and farmer, he was one of four children in a Jewish family. The family moved to Berlin in 1905 and Kurt studied at the universities in Munich and Berlin. He obtained a Ph.D. in psychology on his return to academia after military service in the First World War. With the rise of Hitler, Lewin moved to the United States in 1933, and became a naturalised citizen in 1940.

Lewin devoted most of his career to applied research and practical theory, developing the device of 'action research' in the study of social behaviour (Lewin, 1946). He pioneered work in the area of group dynamics and jointly founded the *Journal of Human Relations*. He died in 1947 in Massachusetts of a heart attack.

Lewin described change as a three-part process. First, there has to be a movement away from the status quo of the current way of thinking and acting. In order to accept change there has to be at least a willingness to change; an understanding of the need to take a new path. This stage, that he called 'Unfreezing', echoes Taylor's view that employees being asked to make improvements in the efficiency of their working practices should be persuaded of the benefits of that change. Once a momentum for change has been established the next phase is one of transition that he called 'Change'. This second phase involves not just the practical aspects of the change, such as adopting new operating procedures or a more efficient IT system, but making the emotional transition to a new environment. The new environment may involve working with new colleagues, and changes to working hours or surroundings; changes that people often find more challenging than the practical ones.

The third and final part of the process Lewin called 'Freezing' (also referred to as 'Refreezing') is where the change is locked in to the everyday working patterns and behaviours of the organisation. Lewin acknowledges that maintaining changes in levels of performance can be challenging with a return to the old ways likely as the initial excitement of the new world fades to being routine. Organisational life in the twenty-first century is more than ever one of continuous change rather than the discrete episodes of a century ago. The 'Freezing' phase then becomes more one of fixing the new levels of performance as the norm from which to move to the next. The three phases of change in Lewin's model now tend to be overlapped by each other in the ongoing process of improvement that characterises modern life. His model though continues to stand. Seen as a series of battles in an ongoing war rather than a sequence of singular events.

As a quick search of the internet will demonstrate, Kurt Lewin's model has spawned numerous mainstream theories on change management. The number of stages in these models varies and the depth of issues addressed at each stage has increased but the basic theory has remained.

All these models focus on the process of change by viewing it as a linear sequence of activities leading from one state to another. Typically, these models set out a process of change management in a sequence of defined stages, such as the following:

1   Assess the options for change
2   Determine the strategy for change
3   Define a change plan
4   Execute the plan
5   Consolidate the change.

In this model, stages 1 and 2 align to Lewin's 'Unfreeze' stage, including defining the intended change and why it is required, setting a clear vision of the future state and setting goals to be achieved by the change.

Stages 3 and 4 are designed to deliver the change. To make the 'transition' from the current practice to the one defined by the first stage.

Finally, stage 5 'freezes' the organisation into the new state. The new ways of working are established as best practice, reinforcing the idea that this is a better way and transferring ownership from the change managers to the employees who are now living in the new way.

In this sort of approach, there is a very strong emphasis on the need for project management of the change process. The impact of the proposed change is assessed. A strategy to deliver the change is formulated. Communication of the need for change is planned. How to effect the change is set out, programmed and how to monitor delivery of the plan is set. The approach is rooted in the systems view of organisations as entities that can be designed and manipulated through some form of external process to bring about a desired future state. Whilst cultural aspects and the willingness of stakeholders to accept change are acknowledged, they are approached on the basis of ensuring that the benefits of change are effectively communicated in order to eliminate resistance.

Resistance to change

Frederick Taylor firmly believed that the case for improving working procedures in the pursuit of efficiency was self-evident. Provided the benefits that would accrue for both the employee and the employer were fully explained and understood by the employee, then he or she would willingly change their way of working to gain the efficiency improvements. Adam Smith's influential work, *An Inquiry into the Nature and Causes of the Wealth of Nations* (Smith, 1977 [1776]) more than a century before established the notion of rational self-interest of individuals in seeking improvement. So it would appear reasonable to assume that faced with the opportunity to gain from improved efficiency, any employee would actively support changes. Similarly, if organisations are rational in seeking to maximise profits, the opportunity to improve returns by changing working methods and procedures should be willingly embraced. The seemingly irrational resistance to change, however, is the most significant issue in the failure to deliver successful change programmes. Taylor viewed such resistance as a failure of communication by those proposing change, leading to lack of understanding of the benefits by those being required to change.

Contemporary thinking on managing change also sees resistance to change in terms of a failure in communication, either in the effectiveness of the message or some form of misinterpretation of that message by those being asked to change. Reasons for resistance to change include the failure, through the way that the message is presented, to engage with the listener. Employees don't see the relevance of the change to them or the need to 'take it on board'. Alternatively, the information put forward triggers a negative emotional response in the recipient. So, it is not the content or the presentation that is at fault, but the recipient. The problem is with him or her, not the messenger! In more abstract terms resistance can be passed off as 'change fatigue' arising from too many successive change initiatives happening too quickly or a lack of mental capacity to deal with learning new ways of working, although the change is thought of as potentially being good.

The process of overcoming resistance is commonly termed as going through the change cycle. This is the sequence of emotional states that are associated with dealing with personal traumas such as bereavement, redundancy or marital breakdown. The first reaction is one of shock, that sudden realisation that your life is about to change radically and a sense of sudden loss. This is followed by a period of denial, the sense that it is not really happening to you. In a bereavement or breakup, that is, there may be an irrational belief that when you get home your loved one will be there and everything will be all right again. Gradually awareness creeps in and you begin to realise that it is actually happening and that things have changed or are about to change. This leads to a sense of acceptance that you are going to have to change and find a way of living with the new circumstances. Acceptance of the inevitability of the change leads to a period of testing where you start to experiment with life in a changed world. Maybe going out on your own or meeting some new people, thinking how it might be to follow a different career path, or what it might be like to take on a new role. Out of that process, eventually, comes an understanding of your new situation. You have learned a new way of being.

It is generally acknowledged that this process is far from being as cut and dried as the description of it would suggest. People will progress through it at differing rates. Some will get 'stuck' at certain points and not be able to move on. This can often be the case with the denial phase, when people are unable to progress to awareness and acceptance and, as we saw in Jim's story, remain convinced that the change will never actually happen and keep their heads firmly planted in the sand. People going through the process can also regress. For example, when they find acceptance a bit too stressful, falling back into the security of denial.

In change management theory, this sequence is viewed very much as a linear process through which people should be managed to overcome the resistance to change and successfully lock in the new ways. Managers are advised to acknowledge that change takes time, that people need to work their way through the cycle; to work with people to co-create the future, help them through the testing phase, and actively create the new ways of working. This way of thinking and working with a changing sequence of feelings in the cycle sustains the scientific management approach. It fits with Lewin's sequence of unfreezing, changing and refreezing. Unfreezing in the phases of shock, awareness and acceptance. Flagging an end to the old ways and creating a willingness to change. Implementing the change through the testing and understanding stages by introducing the new ways and experimenting with them to create a personal understanding of them. Then finally refreezing the organisation by the integration of the changes into everyday life.

Leadership

The work of Taylor and those who have followed in his footsteps has defined change management in terms of a process. A sequence of planned events to put in place and gain compliance with a new way of working and behaving. However, the one essential ingredient without which, in the conventional view, any change programme will fail, is leadership, and in particular strong, or maybe effective, top-down leadership. The view of what is required of an effective leader, one that can set the direction and carry through a change programme, is deeply ingrained in the human psyche. Thinking on leadership, and what makes a good leader, dates back millennia. However, in the study of management and theories of how to bring about business improvement it is a relatively modern phenomenon.

In the fifth century BCE, the Greek philosopher Socrates took what would now be termed a 'transformational view' of leadership. He believed that we are all born with knowledge within us and it is the duty of leaders to bring out the truth for the betterment of society. Unfortunately, this view was restricted to the elites in society rather than the workers. Nevertheless it was an enlightened approach. In the succeeding century, Aristotle believed that everyone is born with a purpose and a function in life. Those who could fulfil their potential for that role would achieve happiness. So, it was the purpose of leadership to create an environment of openness, constructive dialogue and respect and a recognition of values that unite rather than divide. In doing so they would provide opportunities for people to develop their skills and the disciplines required to achieve happiness and a virtuous life. It is this view of leadership that we will return to later as we develop an alternative view of change. But in the meantime, we turn to what has become the dominant view of leadership over the intervening centuries.

On 8 August 1588, having inspected her troops mustered at Tilbury to resist a threatened Spanish invasion, Queen Elizabeth I addressed them saying: 'I know I have the body but of a weak and feeble woman, but I have the heart and stomach of a King, and of a King of England.' This famous speech underlines the long-held view that strong leadership was an exclusively masculine phenomenon. She entreats her soldiers not to see her as a woman, albeit the queen, but as a man and especially as a king. On that day she was clothed in a white dress, but wore over that a silver breastplate to convey masculinity and strength. This understanding of leadership from a military point of view, the embodiment of strength and purpose, the ability to get things done, found its way into the world of industry and business. As the study of leadership developed in the early twentieth century, this assumption was taken almost for granted and the focus was not on what leaders should do but on what characteristics were needed to be a good leader. So, what was required of a leader to make him or her a great one was not in doubt. The question was, what were the characteristics or traits that one might observe in a person that would indicate the potential to be a great leader. The answers to that question, arising from numerous studies, were, or perhaps still are, numerous and varied. However, the most commonly suggested traits of a good leader are given as intelligence and self-confidence.

As the twentieth century progressed and theories of leadership began to take account of the relationship between a leader and those being led, the focus shifted – first, to the style of leadership and then to the way that leaders and their followers interact. The styles of leadership described range from auto-cratic at the military-based end of the scale, to democratic at the consensual end. All of the styles identified, though, still focus on the form of leadership that is imposed upon the followers. Contingency theories of leadership, developed in the later part of the century, are (as their name suggests) contingent on the nature of the relationship between the leader and his or her followers. For example, the identification of leaders as charismatic, rather than being a description of the individual, relates to the ability of the leader to fulfil a need of his or her followers: an ability to deliver them, in some way, from adversity or take them to the promised land. Transformational leadership is defined as the approach that encourages followers to achieve their innate potential, being perhaps the closest form to the philosophy of Aristotle.

Whatever theory you take to be most appropriate, after many decades of observation and research, the view is that leadership is essentially what someone who has assumed that role does in relation to their followers. As with the process of change management, leadership is something that is done to those who are required to change. Effective change management requires strong leadership from the top of the organisation. Leaders are expected to have a clear vision of what the new way of working should be and to be able to communicate that in a clear, unambiguous way such that everyone can understand and identify with it. This is not to say that this 'conventional' view is entirely wrong. Organisational change initiatives will always require, at some point, that the nature of the required change is defined. Implementation of that change will involve some degree of planning to put it in place. It is not sustainable to suggest that, for example, introducing a new computer system or a set of new working procedures does not need to be planned, communicated and trained.

It is, though, how we manage the acceptance of change and enable those affected by it to make the choice to change, that I suggest should be approa-ched from an alternative understanding. How do the individuals involved, who are being asked to change, choose to take that new direction?

We have seen in this chapter, and in Jim's story from Chapter 1, how the managed approach to change has developed out of the tradition of scientific management and is applied to contemporary change management practice; how organisations are viewed, in this tradition, 'as-if' they are a form of mechanistic system that can be manipulated to deliver increased efficiency and performance improvement in general. Taylor's personal views on the self-evidence of acceptance, when it comes to the benefits for all, have remained in the past. We do now acknowledge the emotional roots of resistance to change. However, the common response to resistance assumes that there has been some form of systemic failure. In the next chapter we will explore an alternative view of organisations, one based on what is actually happening in them and how an understanding of complexity theory can enable a different understanding of change in organisations.

References

Lewin, K. 1946. Action Research and Minority Problems. *Journal of Social Issues* 2: 34–46. http://dx.doi.org/10.1111/j.1540-4560.1946.tb02295.x

Lewin, K. 1947. Frontiers in Group Dynamics: Concepts, Method and Reality in Social Science; Social Equilibria and Social Change. *Human Relations* 1: 5–41.

Senge, P. M. 1990. *The Fifth Discipline*. Century Business: London.

Smith, A. 1977 [1776]. *An Inquiry into the Nature and Causes of the Wealth of Nations*. University of Chicago Press: Chicago, Illinois.

Taylor, F. W. 1911. *The Principles of Scientific Management*. Harper and Row: New York.

Vaihinger, H. 1911. *Philosophy of 'As-If: A System of the Theoretical, Practical and Religious Fictions of Mankind*. Meiner: Germany.

3 A complexity view of change

An alternative approach

We have seen in Chapter 2 how Taylorism led to a view of change management that sees organisations 'as-if' they are mechanistic, systems-based, entities. Entities that can be reduced to their component parts and manipulated by some form of applied process to move them from a current to a future state. Based on this premise we tend to think of organisations 'as-if' they are sentient: able to think independently, make decisions and take responsibility. Whilst we know logically that this is not the case we adopt a language and an assumption that it is. An organisation, whether it is a registered company or some form of association, is a legal construct, able to own assets, employ resources and produce goods and services. It cannot, though, in fact is not able to, reason. It cannot hold values or have an independent culture. Despite this we talk of organisations having a culture, that its employees are expected to uphold, having ethical values and being corporately responsible. However, if we take away the individuals employed by the organisation we are not left with anything that is able to behave in a sentient way.

Formally the term '(an) organisation' is defined as something that is capable of transforming an input of resources in materials, people and energy into an output of goods and services. The key part of that process being the ability of the people employed to organise themselves and their resources to form the goods and services. That organising will involve physical activity such as constructing buildings and machinery, moving materials, forming and delivering the completed goods and services. Ultimately, though, the act of organising is the result of communication, of all forms, between the individuals involved.

The approach to managing change, developed over the course of the twentieth century, that we explored in Chapter 2, took as its starting point the assumption that there was a model of organisational change that functions 'as-if' it were a system, a system where actions are taken to be rational and generally linear in nature. That is, people act, as Taylor thought to be self-evident, in the best interests of themselves, their organisation and society in general. The assumption of rationality, in itself, implies a linearity of action and reaction and predictability of the outcome. So, in this view change can be planned, communicated and delivered in a sequence of managed activities.

Complexity

In this chapter, we turn to an alternative approach to understanding organisations and dealing with change in that context, one that does not start from an assumption of a certain model and then uses that to predict behaviour; one that does not start with an assumption of the answer but takes observation of what is actually happening as the route to understanding. We start from the knowledge that organisations consist of groups of individuals that are seeking to transform a set of inputs into outputs and thereby generate value. They achieve that, whilst employing various tools and techniques, by communicating with and responding to each other. We know that, as human beings, our interactions with each other, the gestures that we make (both verbal and non-verbal) and the responses we receive are not always proportionate or entirely rational. They are driven by our deeply held feelings, our values and beliefs, and our personal goals. So, in an organisation, as in society in general, we act within a network of connected individuals in a non-linear responsive way. The outcome of all that activity then emerges from that interaction. To understand that and what it says about the management of organisations and change, we need to study the behaviour and characteristics of such networks and our individual realities that drive those interactions.

Following Bertalanffy's lead we open up the understanding to the study of all systems as being open, subject to the influence of their environments and not strictly driven by rationality. Complexity theory evolved, in the 1980s in the United States, from a multi-disciplinary study of the natural sciences. The research, enabled by the growing power of computing, focused on the behaviour of non-linear networks. This work has given us an understanding of the unpredictable and emergent nature of complex systems. So that we can explore how such an understanding can lead us to our alternative view of change, we need to look at what we mean by complexity and what it can tell us about organisations.

The description of something as 'complex' is used commonly to describe it as being complicated, consisting of many closely inter-related parts. It is a measure of how difficult it is to determine how it works or how an outcome is arrived at. The term 'system', as used in this context, moves us away from the mechanistic view of Taylorism and Bertalanffy. Here we are considering the behaviour of networks of individual agents. These are independent entities, be they human individuals, biological creatures or virtual programmes, that react to sets of learned responses, or schemas, and have the ability to learn and adapt to change in their environment and the responses of others.

In scientific terms, the degree of complexity displayed by a system is determined by the length of the shortest algorithm (or sequence of rules) which is needed to define the behaviour of that system (Gell-Mann, 1994). In simpler language, it is a measure of how difficult it is to describe how something works. For example, the computer programme required to simply add two figures together is relatively short compared to that required to carry out all the functions of a numerical spreadsheet. So, the spreadsheet is more complex than an adding machine.

Complexity is then a function of the regularity of a system. A regular pattern is one that is characterised by being constant, repetitive and evenly spaced. So, where regularity is high then the behaviour of that system can be compressed into an algorithm, or a computer programme, which will describe how the system will react to a range of inputs and determine the output. If the regularity is low then the algorithm will become ever longer until it becomes a full description of every individual detail of the system.

We need, perhaps to pause here and consider the difference between linear and non-linear relationships. Mathematically, linear relationships are those that are directly proportional, e.g. $a = 3 \times b$, which could be represented on a graph as a straight line. Non-linear relationships are not directly proportional, e.g. $a = 3 \times b^2$, and would be represented on a graph by a curve. In the context of complexity theory, we are considering the whole range of relationships that may exist in a network, including physical, chemical and emotional. The key aspect is that a linear relationship will produce a proportional and predictable reaction or response whilst a non-linear one will be non-proportional and, importantly, unpredictable or completely unknowable.

So, linear systems that react to clear cause-and-effect relationships have high regularity and can therefore be described by relatively short algorithms. Where the connections within a system are non-linear and non-proportional then the degree of regularity is low, and the algorithm needed to describe the system would have to be impossibly long to deal with the totality of possible outcomes.

The definition of complexity taken by complexity theory is that of networks in which the behaviour is characterised by non-linearity (Mainzer, 1996). Hence the term complexity, in this context, describes the nature of the network rather than a degree of complication. How, then, does this view inform our understanding of organisations and an approach to change?

Peter Senge (1990), as we saw in Chapter 2, describes systems thinking as a conceptual framework, a body of knowledge and tools, developed over the past fifty years, to make the full patterns of behaviour clearer, and allow them to be changed. The approach of systems theory is based in the application of cause and effect, derived from a reductionist viewpoint of analysis; it is concerned with the nature of relationships. Organisations are seen as goal-seeking feedback systems that adapt to their environments using negative feedback. They work in a logical way towards a defined outcome, making adjustments to that course along the way. An effective organisation is seen as self-regulating, an automatic feature flowing from the way the control system is structured (Stacey, 1993). In this respect, an organisation is presumed to be predictable in its behaviour such that it can be monitored and controlled to move towards specified objectives. The present state can be measured and their processes and behaviour adjusted to achieve a desired future state. Change in a systems theory approach is the result of external influences applied to the system of the organisation. This view assumes that we can fully understand the structure and rules of an organisation and design of a sequence of actions leading to a desired change. The ability to design such a sequence, however, implies both a complete understanding of the behaviour of the system and a linear causality within the components of the organisation. In other words, it is possible to define an algorithm that fully describes the function, relationships and behaviour of an organisation. As-if it was a discrete and independent organism.

Contrary to this, a complexity approach recognises that organisations are composed of highly complex networks of individuals. The relationships between those individuals are non-linear and unpredictable. Defining the behaviour of an organisation by some form of predictive algorithm is impossible. Complexity theory does not start from a need to understand or control its behaviour. It accepts that an organisation is a part of a much wider network of organisations and is, itself, composed of a network of individuals and groups who have their own complex behaviour.

Complex systems

The study of organisations from this perspective is based on observation of how they actually behave rather than seeking to predict that behaviour. Computer simulations, such as those carried out at the Santa Fe Institute, have demonstrated that complex networks will be subject to unpredictable patterns of behaviour that will be self-organising, emergent and inherent in that system. The scientists working at Santa Fe studied what they described as complex adaptive systems wherever they were to be found in nature and drew parallels with human behaviour. It is that work that helps us to understand the nature of complex networks.

A complex adaptive system is one which consists of a network of individual agents. The agents are independent entities that are interacting with each other in accordance with their schema. These are the learned rules that govern their behaviour. The agents in a complex adaptive system may be biological creatures, anywhere from a single-cell organism studied by Kauffman to animals and birds. They can, though, also be replicated in a virtual environment as computer algorithms, or code sequences. What they all have in common is that their behaviour and how they interact with each other is determined by their shared schema. In the case of biological agents that schema has evolved over successive generations. For the agents created in the computer the schema is set into the coding.

Importantly, in the course of their interaction, their learned behaviour will bring them to react to the behaviour of others and to adjust their own actions in the light of that. An example of such behaviour can be seen in the flocking of birds before settling down to roost at night. Each bird flies independently in the flock but will be constantly adjusting its flight according to the path taken by those immediately adjacent to it. The result is an ever-changing flight pattern of the flock that is unpredictable from the behaviour of the individual birds but is recognisable as a complete and unified pattern. Further to that, if the goals of reproduction and survival are added to the schema of the individual agents, you then have the potential of an ecosystem, and over extended periods a process of evolution. Such systems survive by learning and evolving in an adaptive manner, continually adapting their schema in the light of experience (Stacey, 1996a).

The key departure from conventional systems theory is that the behaviour of a complex adaptive system and any emergent phenomenon results from the interaction of the individual agents in the present and not from a pre-set, designed intention. Whilst each agent within the system will have his or her (or its) own intention driven by its schema, the emergent outcome from the system will be unpredictable and changing over time (Stacey, 1996a; Mainzer, 1996).

In 1984 a group of scientists, mostly from the Los Alamos National Laboratory, home of the atomic bomb, and including a number of Nobel Prize winners, founded the Santa Fe Institute in New Mexico, USA. Their objective was to create an environment for research that was not constrained by traditional academic boundaries and where an atmosphere of cooperation and cross-fertilisation of ideas would flourish. Their focus was to take an interdisciplinary research approach in the study of complexity and complex systems.

Stuart Kauffman, an American medical doctor and theoretical biologist, held a faculty in residence at the Santa Fe Institute between 1986 and 1997. He was born in 1939 and educated at Dartmouth in New Hampshire, Oxford University and the University of California. Kauffman's interests and research areas were wide ranging. Whilst at the Santa Fe Institute he specialised in research into the origins of life, gene regulatory networks, developmental biology and the concept of fitness landscapes in evolutionary biology. In 1996 he founded Bois Group, in association with Ernst and Young, to apply complex systems methodology to business problems.

Kauffman's work at the Santa Fe Institute was founded in biology. However, in the cross-disciplinary spirit of the institute, the application of complexity science is across a wide range of areas. He described his work at Santa Fe as the search for the laws of complexity that govern how life evolved from the primeval soup to the biosphere of today (Kauffman, 1995). Encompassing the work of other disciplines including economics, evolution and self-organisation, Kauffman developed a model of the behaviour of complex adaptive systems. He aligns their changing behavioural states with increasing connectivity, as we shall see, and relates this to the concept of fitness landscapes, that we will pick up in Chapter 5.

The cross-disciplinary work of the Santa Fe Institute tends to mirror the nature of complexity by not recognising boundaries set by defined disciplines. A complexity view accepts that everything is connected to some degree with everything else and is influenced in its behaviour by that connection. Thus, the individuals in an organisation are connected to each other locally in their teams or departments. They are also, less directly, connected to all others in the organisation. At the same time, they are closely connected to their family and their friends and beyond that to society in general and ultimately the global community.

So, the study of complexity is related to the behaviour of non-linear networks, whether they are biological, economic, organisational or any other, as all these networks are embedded and interconnected within the overall global network. Indeed, the apparent boundaries used to define these areas are simply artificial notions invented by us to satisfy our desire for order. The connections across these boundaries remain however we define the networks, and they continue to influence the behaviour of all those within the system. Change in one area cannot be divorced from any other and must always then be viewed in the overall context. Similarly, change in any part of an organisation affects everyone in that organisation, its customers and suppliers and the lives of all those connected with it. Equally, it cannot be separated from all the changes that have happened in the past or expectations of change in the future.

The work of Kauffman and his colleagues at the Santa Fe Institute on complexity theory and the behaviour of complex adaptive systems is based on studying systems as a whole and not on breaking them down to analyse the component parts. The development of high-powered computers with sufficient memory capacity to model complex systems over time has enabled researchers to compress the emergent behaviour into manageable timescales (Ray, 1992). The ability of computers to handle vast numbers of calculations at very high speeds enables them to model behaviour of complex networks and represent them graphically.

In 1987 Craig Reynolds, a senior software engineer and academic, simulated the flocking behaviour of birds, along with the herding of animals and the shoaling of fish (Reynolds, 1987: 25–36). Reynolds created computer programmes that gave networks of moving agents the ability to adjust their positions according to fixed rules, in a three-dimensional virtual space, as the position and speed of their neighbours changed. What he was able to demonstrate was that the recognisable flocking patterns of his virtual birds came from each one reacting to its neighbour's position, relative to its own, according to the simple shared set of rules. The flocking patterns were not programmed into the system overall but were emergent from the response of each individual to the movement of its closest neighbours. What these simulations demonstrate is the phenomenon of emergent behaviour and self-organisation in complex networks.

If you have been lucky enough to witness a large flock of birds giving an awesome display of aerial acrobatics when coming down to roost at dusk, you will recall the ever-changing patterns that are formed. As we have seen from the simulations, each bird is responding to those closest to it and changing its course accordingly. The response of each bird to changes in its neighbour's flight path, in a dynamic situation like that, will not be linear. It may accelerate or decelerate, curve one way or the other – all non-linear responses. Their relative positions, how close they are, will affect how strongly or quickly they respond to their neighbours' changes and how many of them they are responding to.

The study of this behaviour in complex systems has found that there is a point where this patterning behaviour emerges. The computer modelling found that there are two factors that influence this. The first is the number of connections that each agent has, i.e. the number of other agents that it is responding to. The second is the strength of the connection, i.e. the degree to which it is influenced by that connection. As these two variables increase a point is reached where an ever-changing creative pattern of behaviour emerges. This is described as the point where the network is operating at, or close to, the 'edge of chaos'.

In this state, the network has reached a condition where the level of connectivity, the strength of response between individuals, is high but not too high and the number of individuals acting in the system is high but not too high. If the connectivity is too low or the number of individuals connected in the system is too low, then the patterns of behaviour will remain stable or unchanging. If the connections or the numbers get too high, then the patterns will become chaotic and unrecognisable, even explosive. Where the conditions are right the network is acting at the 'edge of chaos' and will produce unpredictable but recognisable patterns of behaviour.

In the examples of complex adaptive systems that we have considered so far, the rules of behaviour applied by the agents are relatively fixed. In the natural world, the rules have been modified and developed by natural selection over long periods of time. As human beings, we exist within the same global networks but we have, uniquely, developed the ability to reflect on our actions and to empathise with whom we interact. In a complex adaptive network of human beings, such as those in an organisation, the emergent patterns at the 'edge of chaos' will result from them reflecting on the behaviour of those with whom they interact and modifying their behaviour accordingly. Unlike the virtual birds represented in the computer environment by Reynolds, we are able to learn from our experiences and to modify our behaviour. So the emergent patterns will reflect the ability of the network to learn collectively and to create new, unpredictable, unknowable and novel solutions.

Kauffman (1995: 300), in his work with complexity in the field of biology, draws parallels between the modern organisation and the E coli bacteria, both of which he sees as having the ability to co-evolve with and contribute to the environment in which they exist. Klaus Mainzer (1996), professor of mathematics, physics and philosophy at the University of Munich, also draws on complexity to understand the nature of human society and organisations. He describes society as being characterised by the intention of its members, their own particular schema and goals, whilst governed by the non-linear laws of complexity. He describes how the dynamics of social groups, including organisations, can be seen as adaptive complex systems. The informal structure in organisations, he believes, is achieved though emergent self-organisation; and the wider society, in general, is a highly non-linear, self-referential, system of social networks.

Karl Weick (1995), professor of organisational behaviour and psychology at the Ross School of Business, University of Michigan, whilst not referring directly to the nature of complex adaptive systems, underlines many of the phenomena that drive the behaviour of complex adaptive systems in society and organisations. He describes how individuals make sense of their environment, developing cognitive maps, or schema, continually reflecting on their actions to update their maps, in finding their way. This process of making sense of the world is a circular one of projecting oneself into the environment, observing the consequences and taking one's cue from the conduct of others. It is a complex mixture of proaction and reaction.

Chris Argyris and Donald Schon (1978), in their work on reflective practice, term the learned rules of behaviour, our understanding of the world we live in, as our mental models. They describe a process of continuous revision, in the light of experience, by an individual of these mental models. It is a process of double loop learning where individuals revise their mental models in the face of changes in their environment or unexpected responses to their actions. This description reflects the ongoing change process of action, observation, reflection and change that is part of the continuous development of individual schema within a complex adaptive system.

So far, we have traced the development of an understanding of complex adaptive systems through the behavioural patterns that we observe. In order that we can form a more detailed understanding of that behaviour and how that can inform our view of organisations, we need to take a closer look at their characteristics. We will start with the influence of changing connectivity.

Connectivity

As we have seen, a complex system is any dynamic non-linear network of agents, whose actions, in relation to those that they are connected to, are governed by a set of learned responses or schema. The system is dynamic in that it changes through time in accordance with the schema and is non-linear as the reaction is not necessarily directly proportional to the prompting action. In such a system, each agent behaves in accordance with a set of rules and reacts according to the status of its neighbours. The rules that make up the schema governing the behaviour of the agents are simple logic-type rules, that is 'if – then' decisions which determine how an agent should react based on the status of the agents to which it is connected. In the case of flocking birds, such a rule may be that all the birds will maintain a set distance from each other. So, 'if' two birds get too close to each other, they will 'then' move apart. As they are all following the same rules the whole flock will spread out to accommodate them. Whilst each of the birds is acting independently, in response to the changing relative position of its neighbours, the appearance of the flock will be a changing shape that is emergent from the whole flock.

Imagine that we have a large network of interconnected lightbulbs. The bulbs all share a set of rules that determine the status of each individual bulb according to how many of its neighbours are switched on or off. For example, the status of any particular bulb may be fixed by a rule that says it will be 'on' only if all those bulbs to which it is connected are also 'on'.

Complex systems tend to behave in one of three modes according to the degree of connectivity in the system. At low levels of connection between the agents, where agents are connected to and influenced by one or two of their neighbours, the system settles in to a state of stability. When connectivity between the agents is high, the system remains indefinitely in a chaotic state of random behaviour. Between these two conditions lies the 'edge of chaos'. The transition point between stable and unstable behaviour.

Imagine that the bulbs, in our example, are set out on a large board. At low connectivity, the lights will quickly settle to a fixed pattern. When there is high connectivity the bulbs will continue to flash randomly without any discernible pattern. At the condition of the 'edge of chaos', where connectivity is high but not too high, the lit bulbs will form ever-changing patterns, unpredictable in their nature but recognisable as such.

The degree of connectivity is a function of two parameters: the number of other agents to which any one agent is connected and the probability that any of those connections is likely to bring about change in that agent.

The example of the connection given above is biased towards the bulb being 'off' as all the other bulbs to which this particular one is connected are required to be 'on' for it to be 'on'. The opposite case of the bulb only remaining 'off' when all connected bulbs are also 'off' is equally biased to it being 'on'. In these two conditions, the likelihood is that the bulb will remain in a stable state, either always on or always off. Changing the nature of the rule will, however, tend to make the status of the bulb less predictable. If the rule is changed such that the bulb can be 'on', if just one of its neighbours is 'on' regardless of the status of all the others, then it is equally likely that the bulb will be either 'on' or 'off'. As the degree of predictability declines, the pattern of lit bulbs becomes chaotic with no discernible patterns. As the network moves from a stable orderly state to the chaotic random state, it passes through the boundary condition of being at the 'edge of chaos' (Kauffman, 1995). In this state, at the 'edge of chaos', the network of lit bulbs settles into ever-changing but recognisable patterns.

In this example of the effect of changing connectivity, the state of the connected bulbs is limited to being either on or off. The rules determining the status of the bulbs is linear, if – then, in nature and predictable. However, when we come to consider networks of individuals in society and organisations, the way they react to each other is nonlinear and unpredictable. The strength of the connection and the probability of bringing about change in one individual by another will depend on the influence one has over the other.

Emergence

The light patterns that we see in the bulbs as the degree of connectivity increases is an emergent quality of the network. The large network of inter-connected bulbs in this example is complex, as we defined earlier, and the rules governing the status of the bulbs are fixed. In a complex adaptive system, however, the agents are able to learn from their experience and adapt their responses accordingly. The agents in such a system are not purely reacting blindly to the status of their neighbours, they are constantly reconstructing the world in which they exist in order to achieve their objectives. The objectives can be both individual and shared. Individual objectives could be personal survival or the accumulation of resources. Shared, collective or system objectives may be reproduction, for the survival of the group or the performance of some joint task, as in an organisation.

We can explore the phenomenon of emergence in a complex adaptive system by thinking about the behaviour of traffic on a motorway as the density of that traffic increases. When traffic is light each car's driver acts relatively independently of the other driver's behaviour. All the drivers have the common objective of progressing along the motorway at a steady pace of their choosing and arriving safely at their destination. Equally, all drivers' behaviour is controlled by a shared set of rules that govern the basic manoeuvres that they follow and determine the expectations of others as to that behaviour. In light traffic the connectivity is low with the reactions of each driver being affected by only one or two others. The reaction times required are longer and therefore behaviour is stable and more predictable.

As traffic density increases, however, the level of connectivity rises. Each driver has to interact with a larger number of other vehicles. Distances between vehicles are reduced, reaction times lessened and the predictability of other drivers' actions lessens. Changes in the rules governing the interaction between the vehicles are now needed. The need to adjust speeds to that of the vehicle in front rather than overtaking is added to the schema. The rules of behaviour have to be adapted to take account of traffic moving at differing relative speeds in adjacent lanes. The increasing density of traffic causes the behaviour of the traffic to change from an orderly and stable flow to what eventually becomes a disordered state where little or no progress is made and the objectives are unattainable. Between these two states there is a boundary condition where the flow is neither stable and orderly nor completely stationary. At this point patterns of movement emerge where the speed of flow varies in a longitudinal wave formation. In this situation, the individual drivers are learning on a continuing basis how to deal with the flow of the traffic around them, constantly rearranging their behaviour with respect to the surrounding vehicles with whom they are interacting in pursuit of the overall objective of safe passage.

The system represented by this example is a complex adaptive system; it consists of a network of connected agents that share a set of rules governing both their behaviour in motorway driving and the individual rules of survival and progress. The state of the system varies with increasing connectivity and reducing predictability of behaviour, displaying self-organising patterns of density along its length as it nears the boundary condition at the 'edge of chaos'. In common with other complex systems this example is sensitive to small changes or perturbations in the system, often with dramatic consequences – where a relatively insignificant event, maybe a momentary distraction, can rapidly escalate to a major incident.

The wave pattern of traffic accelerating and slowing on the crowded motorway is a function of the complex adaptive system of interaction between the drivers of the vehicles. The pattern is not explicit in the individual drivers' intentions or their schema. The pattern is emerging from the behaviour of the system as a whole. The effect of self-organisation is an emergent phenomenon of that complex adaptive system rather than any of the individual agents.

Finally, in our understanding of the behaviour of complex systems, we turn to the role of attractors and the characteristic of self-similarity.

Attractors and self-similarity

Complex systems are sensitive to initial conditions. That is, the status of the system at the outset will determine the behaviour of the system from that point on.

In our light bulb example, each light bulb is reacting to the status of the other light bulbs that it is connected to. That determines whether it lights up or not. So, the emerging pattern or patterns of lit bulbs evolves over time. The starting condition is then important. Which bulb lights up first when the power is applied will determine how the patterns progress from there. Any slight change in that initial condition will result in a completely different sequence of patterns. Any interference in the network, such as the failure of a bulb to light when it should will send the network into a changed pattern.

This is the effect known generally, in chaos theory, as the butterfly effect. It is the idea that the movement of a butterfly's wing can develop, in due course through the progression of the complex system that is the earth's weather system, to a hurricane in another part of the globe. Here a small change in a part of the system can be magnified by the chain of interaction and positive feedback (characteristic of non-linear systems) with other parts of the system to cause dramatic patterns to build.

In our example, if the degree of connectivity is high the behaviour of the system will be unpredictable due to the large number of factors which can affect each change, stability will be low, and dramatic self-organising patterns will result. However, if the connectivity is low the relationships will be more predictable and the system is more stable. In this condition, the system will either freeze into a stable state, where the pattern of the lit bulbs becomes constant after a short sequence of adjustment, or it will settle into an ongoing sequence of repeated patterns. Where you have repeated patterns the conditions that determine the particular sequence taken up by the system are known as attractors.

If we consider the way animals change the way they move we see the effect of an attractor. An example of this is the changing gait of a horse as it increases its speed of movement from walking to trotting and on to galloping. The patterns of motion are tending towards a state of lowest energy consumption and as the pace is increased the pattern changes from one cycle of leg movements to another. Each gait is drawn by an attractor of movement for lowest energy at that pace.

The complex system that is the horse has evolved by adaptation of the schema or rules governing its movement, to a position of lowest energy use in motion. This has given it an advantage over its adversaries, and indeed a special relationship with man, which has ensured its survival. Its system of movement is sensitive enough to have a number of individually stable attractors of movement without it becoming chaotic. The system operates at a position of sensitivity, determined by its connectivity, which is stable but at the same time responsive enough to changes. This allows the system to switch from one self-organised pattern to another, that is, it is operating at the 'edge of chaos'.

When we think of an attractor, in this context, we are talking about a condition, a state of being, rather than some form of physical attraction like magnetism. In the changing gait of a horse as its pace increases, the change ensures that the animal exerts the least amount of effort for that speed. In this case the attractor is the condition of lowest energy expended. Other attractors may be the equilibrium of temperature, a balance of applied forces or, as in the complex global weather systems, conditions of lowest air pressure.

So, we have seen how the behaviour of a complex adaptive system moves from stable to chaotic as the connectivity within the system is increased. As the system moves towards the 'edge of chaos' it moves to a cycle of repeated patterns of behaviour. At lower levels of connectivity, the number of cycles will also be short and the patterns stable. With rising connectivity, the cycle of patterns lengthens until, as the system approaches a chaotic state, the duration of the cycle will tend to infinity. Systems that are operating in a stable regime close to the 'edge of chaos' will display patterns of behaviour which are unpredictable but recognisable. The exact pattern will not be repeated but will have properties of self-similarity with the preceding patterns. Mandelbrot (1977) recognised the phenomenon of self-similarity in what he described as the fractal nature of patterns. Fractal patterns are free of scale, often appearing at varying magnitudes embedded within themselves. Think of the shape of the coast on a map. As you focus in, seeing headlands and inlets in greater detail, the pattern is similar and repeated. Such, self-similar patterns can be seen in the nature of structures arising from complex systems in the appearance of living systems. In the same way, the structures of trees are all unique, individual in their detail but all have self-similarity. They are all recognisable by their tree-like appearance and fractal in that a twig resembles a branch, in shape and structure, and the branch resembles the tree. Similarly, the exact appearance of the human face is never repeated but all are recognisable.

Ralph Stacey (Stacey, 1996a: 37, 43), writing on complex adaptive systems, describes how 'life in organisations is continuously unfolding in irregular patterns of a self-similar nature at all levels and over all time frames'. The similarities within the behavioural patterns through the various levels and groupings become the shared schema of the organisation. That shared schema will change over time as the embedded systems develop.

With an understanding of the characteristics of complex systems we can look at organisations from this perspective. Observing the behaviour in organisations and in society as a whole, we see how these characteristics play out daily. Paying attention to what is actually happening we see that events and behaviours are emerging around us from our everyday interactions. A change of mood, a change in the degree of formality of dress has emerged. New forms of expression come in to fashion and then fade away again. Changes in opinions come about, moving from left to right of the political spectrum. Whilst there was no consciously made decision to adopt the new way, no consultation between the members of the organisation, a new understanding of what is acceptable has come about. How often do we say 'I don't know where that came from' when we suddenly become conscious that things have changed?

We see behaviours and opinions forming that are drawn to certain attractors. Probably one of the most powerful attractors in the area of change is that of the status quo. As with the gait of the horse in motion we are drawn to the route of least energy. Maintaining the current way of doing things seemingly requires the least amount of effort. We don't have to learn anything new. There is no effort required in changing current habits or having to find a new status quo. Ironically, this generally results in the expenditure of energy in a different way in the resistance of the change. A culture of resistance emerges which becomes the new norm.

Power and reward also provide powerful attractors for emergent behaviour. Status derived from one's position in the organisation, the office that you occupy or the car that you drive, the people who are in your circle of influence and who you know, are all powerful drivers of behaviour and as such attractors. The patterns of behaviour that emerge will be different as the interactions between individuals develop and will constantly be changing and unpredictable. At the same time, though, they will be recognisable. We all recognise the behaviours that go with a refusal to accept change: non-cooperation, expressing belief in the new way but then keeping to the old. The patterns of emerging behaviour have self-similarity – always different but recognisable for what they are.

Wilfred Ruprecht Bion, the influential twentieth-century British psychoanalyst who rose to become president of the British Psychoanalytical Society in the 1960s, defined a series of behavioural patterns in groups of individuals that he termed Basic Assumption Behaviour. His work was in the study of group behaviour and the unconscious behaviours that emerge in a group's response to feelings of stress and anxiety. He referred to them as Basic Assumption Behaviours because they are deeply rooted and appear to be an assumed response by the group as a whole. By applying an understanding of complexity theory, we can see these behaviours as emergent and driven by the attractor of reducing anxiety and stress.

Bion (1961) identified three basic assumption behaviours: dependency, fight or flight, and pairing. Of these, the first two are the most commonly recognised. Anyone that follows political life, in any country, will be familiar with these. When anxiety and stress levels rise, particularly when livelihoods and status are threatened by the pending elections or in the aftermath of an election defeat, we see in-fighting. We see people distancing themselves from the result or from policies that they once held but now appear to be unpopular. Dependency is where there is a compulsion to find, or replace a leader, often after an electoral failure or where the prospect of success appears to be dwindling. The search at the basic level is to find someone or something, maybe a new policy, that will take away the stress and anxiety and make everything better again. The expectation placed by the group on such a leader is generally unsustainable and inevitably the new leader will be seen to fail and will be brought down by the very people who put them there. Very few political leaders leave office at the time of their own choosing and on a high of support. Bion's work and that of the Tavistock Institute of Human relations has shown that these behaviours are driven by unconscious feelings communicated, usually non-verbally, between members of the group. The behaviours are unpredictable as to which one will be followed and emergent from the group. At the same time, they will be recognisable within the definitions set out. That is, they are emergent, self-similar and driven by the attractor of lower stress and anxiety.

Change as a complex process

We can now see change, and the reaction to change, as a complex process rather than a managed and externally directed activity. The key to understanding how this process works and what drives the emergence of change and our response to it lies in the ongoing way in which we make choices and react to our environment. For that, we need to turn to the most complex and common system of all, our brain and how we make those choices. To do that, we will consider the work of George Herbert Mead and the advances in the study of neuroscience.

Mead was born on 27 February 1863, in Hadley, Massachusetts, into a strongly Protestant family. His father came from a lineage of farmers and clergyman and was professor of theology at Oberlin College, Ohio, where George's mother also taught. Mead also graduated from Oberlin and later studied at Harvard and in Liepzig, Germany. After short spells as a teacher and a railroad surveyor, Mead moved into academia in 1891, working at the

University of Michigan before moving to the University of Chicago in 1894. He died of heart failure in Chicago in 1931.

Mead was recognised as a philosopher, sociologist, and psychologist and regarded as one of the founders of social psychology. He was a prodigious writer of articles and reviews; however, much of his work, in the form of books, was published posthumously by a group of students who put together his lecture notes to produce four influential volumes of work between 1932 and 1938. Strongly influenced by Albert Einstein's work on relativity and Darwin's on evolution, Mead struggled for many years, caught between his secular education and his Christian upbringing and beliefs. His thinking ranged across a wide spectrum from social behaviour to the nature of the self and the development of the mind. In our consideration of complexity, we will focus on two particular areas. Further on, as we discuss human interaction, we will look at his work on communication and the emergence of meaning though language. Here we will follow his interest in relativity and perhaps one of his less celebrated works on how individuals act in the moment.

In his book published by his students in 1932 (Mead, 1932a), he reasoned that the future is perpetually constructed in what he termed the 'specious present' (now more commonly termed the 'living present'), where action in the immediate present is continually formed and reformed by the experience of the past and by the present expectation of the future (Stacey, 2001: 173). So for each of us the meaning ascribed to any situation and the action we take, in the present, is constantly being formed and reformed by our interaction with those around us, our environment and our internal selves. Mead's view was that we are all influenced in the way we act in the present by a combination of our perception of our past experience and our expectation of what the future will hold.

It is important here to note that our memory of the past is not fixed, as in the nature of a collection of photographs or videos, but is constantly revised by our ongoing reflection on our experience. So, we re-evaluate the past in the light of the present. Thinking back, we are all familiar with the idea that the summers of our childhood were endless sunny days. They weren't but they are the ones that made the most impression and we adjust our perceptions in the light of what we experience today: more than likely cool and damp! More seriously, as children or young adults we form opinions of our parents based on the reality, as we see it at the time. We maybe saw them as being too overbearing and restrictive in what they allowed us to do. Perhaps you saw them as being overly critical of the younger generation and you in particular. Alternatively, you may have thought that they were not interested enough, not helping you to grow and develop. Often as we grow up, we vow not to make the same mistakes, as we saw them, when we become parents. However, as we mature and perhaps take on the role of parenthood our perceptions change. Experience allows us to re-evaluate the past as our reality changes. We perhaps understand better what they were doing and why. As our reality evolves so does our view of how we got to where we are.

Mead's thinking was influenced by his interest in developments in early twentieth-century brain research. At that time the subject was in its very early stages of understanding, and Mead's was mainly interested in observing social interaction. He was particularly focused on the role that the brain and the central nervous system might play in anticipating future actions. At this stage of understanding, the role of conscious thought was predominant and assumed to be the driver of behaviour. Mead passed away in the early 1970s as the explosion in computing power was getting underway. The revolution in computing and the memory capacity that made simulations of complex systems possible has also opened up the study of the brain and advanced our understanding of memory through neuroscience. Using neuroimaging we are able to identify areas of activity in the brain under particular conditions. Whilst we cannot, at this stage, map the immense number of neurons in the brain and the seemingly endless number of potential connections between them, we can see which parts of the brain are responding to certain stimuli.

Creating a personal reality

We now understand that there are differing forms of memory, held by forming patterns of connections between neurons that reside in different areas of the brain. For example, the cerebellum at the base of the brain closest to the top of the spinal cord, the part of the brain known as the hindbrain, stores learned actions associated with movement such as kicking a football. This form of memory is part of the wealth of unconscious or implicit memory that enables us to function without having to think about it. Imagine the energy that would be needed if we had to think about breathing all the time. If we had to remember to put one foot in front of the other in order to be able to walk across a room. As we saw in the example of the horse's changing gait as its speed increases, our brains are drawn to the attractor of lowest energy. By burning the memory of how to carry out everyday repetitive tasks into our unconscious brain we don't have to think about it (Eagleman, 2011: 72). In fact, the vast majority of our actions and the decisions that we make are controlled by the areas of our brain that we do not have conscious access to, the store of memory that allows us to function without conscious thought.

The evolution of the human race has provided us with a basic starter kit of memory: those actions that ensure survival, the implicit knowledge that drives basic functions such as breathing and eating but also an attraction to a smiling face that draws us to our parents for protection. This form of genetic memory is then built on as we construct our reality and figure out how the world works. Infants build on that initial memory, creating their particular version of the reality that they experience by exploring the world. As they learn how to navigate their world, working out how what they see enables them to avoid bumping into things, knowing the difference between a pleased expression and one of disapproval, the knowledge is hardwired into the unconscious brain. As adults, we learn to drive and repeated practice means that we can travel to work without even being aware of when and how to change gear. When learning to play a musical instrument, we commit the skills to our unconscious memory to enable us to interpret the music to the point that where thinking about what we are doing becomes unproductive – that is the point where it all goes wrong rather than getting better.

The ancient Greeks believed that we see by emitting rays from our eyes that enable us to scan the world around us. This belief is cemented into our language by the term 'looking' being an active verb, something that we do. We now understand that the opposite of that is what actually happens. We are the passive receivers of a stream of photons that are emitted by the things that are in our field of vision. What we experience as 'sight' is a pattern of neural firing in our brain that is stimulated by the electronic pulses coming from the retina in response to those photons. The reality that we build in response to those patterns is how we understand and navigate the world around us.

The reality that each of us creates is unique. It is an unanswerable question as to whether what you experience as the colour red is the same as I experience. What we do know is that particular types of photons emanate from something that we acknowledge as being coloured red. Those photons enter the eye and stimulate receptors in the retina and an electronic signal is sent to the brain. A pattern of neural firing is produced in the memory that matches that experienced previously as the colour red. By common agreement we ascribe the colour red to that experience. The version of reality that each of us constructs and holds in our unconscious brain is dependent on our personal experience from birth. That experience is necessarily unique to every individual and therefore different. As Mead suggested, our personal reality is not static. We are continually experiencing new things and the reality stored in our unconscious brain is constantly updated. Family, neighbourhood, colleagues and the media all influence our perceptions of reality. So, that perception of our past and the actions and decisions we make in the living present, driven by that reality, is constantly revised.

Surely though, we are free to make decisions about how we act based on rationality? We have a conscious brain and it is the 'we', that is our conscious thoughts. The thoughts that decide what we do.

Deciding to act

The way we act and the decisions we make, in Mead's living present, is driven by our perception of our past, and also by our expectation of the future. This is where the conscious part of the brain comes into play. Located in the two frontal lobes, in the forebrain, the conscious brain is where we build our vision of the future. The part, unique to the human brain, that enables us to be able to reflect on our existence. Clearly, we cannot predict the future but we can, based on our past experience, consider what we expect of the future. We can weigh up the risks and advantages of alternative futures and act towards that position. The memory of past experience, that we build up over the years, influences how we respond to each potential future state. If there is a plan to go on holiday but your dominant memory of past holidays is of it being cold, wet and miserable rather than warm, sunny and enjoyable, then your reaction to that plan, however promising it may sound, will be influenced by that association. In our example of the motorway traffic, how we interact with the other traffic, or more specifically the other drivers, is driven by our unconscious, hardwired, memory of past experience – the experience of being driven by our parents when we were young, how we learnt to drive and all the near, or maybe not so, near-miss accidents over the years. All of these experiences motivate the way we interact, the decision to overtake or brake, speed up or slow down. All of them are taken unconsciously in the living present.

So, our expectation draws on past, largely unconscious memories combined with the conscious reasoning that this time it may be different. We all make plans for our careers. Imagining what it would be like to be a nurse or an engineer. Maybe we yearn to be an Olympic athlete or a tennis champion. We can plan a route to that ambition and study or train for it in an effort to achieve it. That studying and training will ultimately revise the reality held in the unconscious as it becomes a part of our past. So, in this way, the role of the conscious brain is to deal with the unexpected that we experience as we move into the future, to figure out the new reality posed by that new experience and, in the pursuit of the lower energy state of automated reactions, commit that reality to the unconscious brain.

Neuroscience expresses Mead's perception of the past and expectation of the future as the implicit and explicit attitudes respectively. How we act in the present is driven by the conjunction of these two attitudes. An explicit desire to learn to swim is maybe constrained by an implicit fear of water, buried deep in the unconscious. How that plays out in any individual depends on the degree to which the conscious brain is able to modify the implicit by making it explicit.

Organisations and complexity

Stepping away from the systems view of organisations towards a complexity perspective, we see organisations as patterns of communicative interaction between independent individuals, or in other words, ongoing conversations, whose future state is constantly emergent. The organisation cannot be isolated from its context, redesigned and then reconnected. Change is a perpetual process that emerges from those conversations and the interactions of the individuals, employees, stakeholders, customers and all those linked to the organisation. Change is a consequence of the collective choices made by these individuals.

In their development of the understanding of complexity, as it applies to organisations, Ralph Stacey and his colleagues at the Complexity Management Centre have taken the behaviour of complex adaptive systems and the study of psychoanalysis to arrive at a theory of Complex Responsive Processes (Stacey, 2001). This is an understanding which focuses on the interaction between individuals in an organisation, not to predict behaviour and manage outcomes, but to allow us to work with the unpredictability and emergent qualities of networks of individuals. In other words, to pay attention to what is actually happening in the organisation, in the sum of all those interactions, and work with that to foster innovation and change.

Stacey grew up in South Africa and later studied at the London School of Economics where he took an MSc. in 1964 and a doctorate in econometric modelling in 1967. He settled in the UK in 1970 and pursued a career in business and corporate management before turning to academia. In 1992 he was appointed Professor of Management at the University of Hertfordshire.

Stacey's work in business, particularly in strategic planning, led him to study the reasons why, as he saw it, conventional scientific approaches to planning and forecasting generally failed (Stacey, 1991: 3). This question has driven his 30-year quest to develop his thinking. His publications have progressed from thinking on scientific chaos to complex adaptive systems and, since the turn of the millennium, in the development of his theory of complex responsive processes.

In parallel with his university work, Stacey trained as a group psychotherapist, qualifying in 1998. As a member of the Institute of Group Analysis and the Group Analytic Society he practised in group clinical therapy until 2004. This work and his involvement with the Tavistock Institute of Human Relations, on group behaviour as a part of the university's MBA programme, informed his thinking on human relating in organisations.

Stacey's earlier work drew on complexity science and the work of Melanie Klein, Donald Winnicott and others in psychoanalysis to develop a model of organisational behaviour and management. He described organisations and groups within organisations as 'nested complex adaptive systems', a series of interlinked networks that extends from the individual human mind to the global social, economic and political systems (Stacey, 1996b). The agents that make up the human mind are the images contributing to the individual's mental model of the world, the individual's schema, which governs his or her actions within the social networks in which the individual acts. Those social networks include the groups and teams within the organisation for whom he or she works which in turn make up the organisation. The organisation is itself an agent acting in the social, economic and political network of the host country and global systems.

The neuroscientific view of this places the hardwired patterns of memory in the unconscious brain as the images making up the individual's mental model, the patterns that make up an individual's reality and determine his or her reactions in the present; reactions that are potentially unpredictable and emergent from the complexity of those patterns. So, the interaction between individuals working within groups and organisations is non-linear. The spontaneous self-organisation and emergence of strategy are demonstrable properties of non-linear feedback. Thus, to understand the nature of complex adaptive systems is to understand the nature of organisations rather than a prescription for their management. The patterning of the firing neurons in the brains of the individuals are the drivers of behaviour for them as the agents within the networks in which they interact.

This view provides us with a way to understand how the patterns of activity in organisations are emergent from the network of individuals working there. Those patterns are not determined by any one individual but are emergent from the collective actions of all the individuals. We can see how those actions are driven, in the choices made in the present, bringing together our past experience and expectation of the future.

However, by taking a view of organisations from the behaviour of complex adaptive systems still leaves us viewing organisations 'as-if' they are such systems. We are able to move away from viewing organisations as being 'a thing', something that is able to think and act independently, to being the emergent and unpredictable outcome of a group of individuals acting together. But thinking of it as a particular type of system still implies the ability to influence the output by external manipulation of that system. We need to get away from the search for the best-fit model for organisations, the ultimate 'as-if' solution, to focus on what is actually happening. To move from an 'as-if' approach to what it 'actually is'. To do that we need to pay attention to what is actually happening rather than what, perhaps, we think ought to be happening.

In 1995 Stacey established a doctoral research group which focused its thinking on complexity theory as applied to organisations. The work of this group produced a number of successful PhD theses and a series of books exploring topics such as change consulting and creativity and innovation in organisations from a complexity perspective. Among the students in the group were Patricia Shaw and Douglas Griffin, who went on with Stacey to found the Complexity Management Centre at the university. Stacey's work with Shaw and Griffin moved their thinking away from complex adaptive systems. They developed their understanding of processes of human relating, known as Complex Responsive Processes. They were working with complexity characteristics, such as emergence and self-organisation, and the thinking of social philosophers such as George Herbert Mead, to draw together the understandings from complexity science and social science.

A key aspect of this development was to start from the simple observation that what is actually happening in organisations is an ongoing sequence of communication. Whilst the context of the organisation remains the same, the physical location and layout do not change and the processes that are followed tend to be constant, what differs every day is the conversation. The sequence of gesture and responses made through our spoken language, our body language and emotions that make up our interpersonal reactions. We have seen in the nature of complex systems the characteristic of self-similarity, where the patterns are always different but at the same time recognisable. In organisations, as in life generally, that phenomenon can be seen. Our days are similar but always different. What makes them different is the changing conversations we have, the differing ways that we interact with each other and the actions that come from that. Small things can escalate into major issues. A minor hold-up on the journey into work that makes us late for a meeting can turn the whole day into a nightmare. A chance remark over coffee that is misinterpreted leads to a lack of cooperation on a sales project and a loss of business. Despite all the plans, policies and procedures, what is actually happening is how we are acting and responding to each other in the present.

To explore this further we can now turn back to Mead and his work on communication and the emergence of language to look at the nature of human interaction.

Communication through gesture and response

Darwin's influence on Mead's thinking led him to link the development of social behaviour to evolution and the human use of tools, facilitated by the nature of the human hand. The ability to use tools gave humans an intimate connection to their environment and the ability to shape it through their actions. Mead saw language as the ultimate tool, something which brought with it the ability to develop intelligence, which in turn allows the further development of those tools. 'Language is [then] a principle of social organisation that has made the distinctly human society possible' (Mead, 1932b: 260). The communication that Mead refers to goes beyond the language of the spoken word. He described communication as an interactive process of gesture and response, a constant sequence of gestures, spoken words, body postures, facial expressions and a whole host of unconscious actions. Mead recognised that these gestures evoke responses which are influenced by our ability to feel the emotions implied by the original gesture. For example, if someone speaks to you in angry tones you will feel that anger and experience a physical response; perhaps a rise in blood pressure or a reddening of the face. This response gesture will in turn be picked up by the original person, and so we have a sequence of gestures and responses, not all spoken, from which a fight may emerge.

Modern neuroscience has identified the presence of mirror neurons in the brain. These are hardwired patterns of neurons that enable us to see the mind state of another person. They work in our unconscious, picking up information about the feelings of others. These are the patterns, recognised from our genetic memory and earliest experiences, that prompt the automatic reaction to a smile. Having recognised the feelings of those around us we tend to mirror that feeling in our own interaction, as in the response to dilated pupils that attracts us to a sexual partner, creating an emotional resonance and behavioural imitation. They are the patterns that drive the dance of gesture and response that connects our internal state with those around us, even without the participation of our conscious mind (Siegel, 2003). It is in this way that we are able to pick up the mood of a group or empathise with the painful feelings of someone in distress. In Bion's basic assumption behaviour we pick up the feeling of anxiety in a group and assume a collective response by experiencing the feelings of the others and communicating that back to the group. The identification of the role of mirror neurons in driving the unconscious process of gesture and response cements Mead's description of the process of emergence in communication and social behaviour.

Stacey and his colleagues have described their theory of complex responsive processes as one of human relating. Mead's work on the emergence of social behaviour from gesture and response is a key concept in that theory. The unpredictable and emergent nature of organisations that Stacey identifies, through his work on complex adaptive systems, is refined by shifting the emphasis from the nature of systems to the emergence of meaning in gesture and response. Organisations are thus seen as self-organising patterns of conversations in which human identities emerge (Stacey, 2003). Individual realities, in the context of the organisation, are constantly formed and reformed. We are now working with what is actually happening in the organisation.

Organisations as they actually are

We have considered the view of organisations that is prompted by the scientific management theory that they act 'as-if' they are discrete systems that can be manipulated when we want to bring about a change in their state, through a process that creates a need to change, implements a new state, perhaps a new way of working or behaving and then cements that into everyday practice. This is a view that tends to treat organisations as a form of sentient organism capable of holding values and a social conscience.

I suggested that if we take away the individuals we are not left with anything that is capable of acting in that way. In the absence of artificial intelligence, without the individuals we only have a collection of buildings, machinery, stock and products. What makes it an organisation is not even just the individuals themselves but the way they interact, and particularly the activity that emerges from that interaction.

We have seen that the insights gained from modern neuroscience help us to understand how Mead's description of acting in the living present through an ongoing sequence of gesture and response creates, in an organisation as with all social groupings, the behavioural patterns described by complexity theory. The personal reality that we build, and constantly rebuild, in our unconscious brain, together with our expectations of the future, are expressed in our gestures and responses in the present. By paying attention to what is actually happening in those organisations we see that the only variable is the ongoing conversation of those gestures and responses.

So, an organisation is a complex network of individuals where each individual is connected in local interactions, in the present, from which patterns of behaviour and activity emerge on an ongoing basis. This view of organisations is supported by the observation of patterns of difference and self-similarity. Life is similar from day to day, but is always different. Life is unpredictable and non-linear as some things escalate seemingly out of nowhere whilst other things that appear at first to be very important fade into insignificance. We are drawn, unconsciously to certain strange attractors such as maintaining the status quo in the face of change as that is the line of least effort. We tend to respond to anxiety, particularly when faced with change, by adopting the attractors of basic assumption behaviour to lower that anxiety. So, if that is what organisations actually are then we need to approach change or the creation of change in an organisation from that perspective rather than that of the systems and scientific management view.

In this chapter we have built an alternative view of organisations and change based on a holistic approach to research and theoretical thinking. In the next chapter we shall see how this approach can be seen to apply to real-life situations. In her story, Ruth reflects on her experience of working with organisations in change and how she encountered unexpected reactions and emergent behaviour.

References

Argyris, C. and Schon, D. 1978. *Organisational Learning: A Theory of Action Perspective.* Addison-Wesley: Reading, MA.

Bion, W. R. 1961. *Experiences in Groups.* Routledge: London.

Eagleman, D. 2011. *Incognito: The Secret Lives of the Brain.* Canongate: Edinburgh.

Gell-Mann, M. 1994. *The Quark and the Jaguar: Adventures in the Simple and the Complex.* Little, Brown: London.

Kauffman, S. 1995. *At Home in the Universe.* Penguin: London.

Mainzer, K. 1996. *Thinking in Complexity: The Complex Dynamics of Matter, Mind and Matter,* 2nd edn. Springer: Berlin.

Mandelbrot, B. 1977. *The Fractal Nature of Geometry.* Freeman: New York.

Mead, G. H. 1932a. *The Philosophy of the Present.* University of Chicago Press: Chicago.

Mead, G. H. 1932b. *Mind, Self and Society.* University of Chicago Press: Chicago.

Ray, T. S. 1992. An Approach to the Synthesis of Life. In G. C. Langton, C. Taylor, J. Doyne Farmer and S. Rasmussen (eds), *As-If Life II.* Santa Fe Institute Studies in the Science of Complexity, vol. 10. Addison-Wesley: Reading, MA.

Reynolds, C. 1987. Flocks, Herds and Schools: A Distributed Behavioural Model. *Computer Graphics* 21: 25–36.

Senge, P. M. 1990. *The Fifth Discipline.* Century Business: London.

Siegel, D. 2003. *Clinical Applications of Interpersonal Neurobiology.* Six-hour CD course, November. https://www2.psychotherapynetworker.org

Stacey, R. D. 1991. *The Chaos Frontier.* Butterworth-Heinemann: Oxford.

Stacey, R. D. 1993. *Strategic Management and Organisational Dynamics.* Pitman: London.

Stacey, R. D. 1996a. *Complexity and Creativity in Organisations.* Berrett-Koehler: San Francisco.

Stacey, R. D. 1996b. *Excitement and Tension at the Edge of Chaos.* Centre for Complexity and Management working paper no. 6, April. University of Hertfordshire Business School: Hertford.

Stacey, R. D. 2001. *Complex Responsive Processes in Organisations.* Routledge: London.

Stacey, R. 2003 Learning as an Activity of Independent People. *The Learning Organisation* 10(6): 325–331.

Weick, K. E. 1995. *Sensemaking in Organisations.* Sage: Thousand Oaks, CA.

4   Facilitating change

A story of change leadership

In taking the approach to viewing organisations set out in Chapter 3, we have emphasised the role of the individual and the importance of paying attention to what is actually going on. We have seen how each individual's choice to change is driven, in the living present, by the deeply held assumptions implicit in our unconscious realities. How the change that actually occurs, or the resistance to change that arises, is emergent from the interaction between the individuals in a complex responsive process. How does that view, though, play out in real life?

In this chapter we hear Ruth's story. Ruth, now an independent business advisor, university lecturer and management researcher, came to managing change in organisations almost by accident. Through a family connection she became involved in a business that was facing the challenges of computerisation and globalisation, and took on the leadership of the company. Without any formal training in change management at that stage, Ruth learned by observation and having to interact with the reactions to change as they emerged.

Unexpected beginnings

"I don't think I ever set out to be a business leader or to be involved in organisational change. Although I did grow up in a family business, my parents ran a theatrical school and the day-to-day problems of managing our own income was a part of that. I didn't see that as a career path. But then life never really pans out the way that you planned it to!

"When I met my husband, he was already the owner and leader of a successful freight forwarding business, P&F Limited. Even then I was not involved in the business beyond my role as his wife and accompanying him on various social occasions from time to time. It was not until our children had grown up and moved on to university that, whilst looking to what I could do with my new found spare time, my husband Paul suggested that I might help out at his company for a while.

"I have always had a great thirst for knowledge and a desire to learn from whatever situation I found myself in. So I guess that is how I now find myself in academia and have the opportunity to draw on the lessons that I have learned through the experience of, eventually, running my husband's business and then building a business of my own in advising small firms in change. Working now in the business school, teaching and doing research, I have the opportunity to reflect on that experience and develop my understanding by drawing on contemporary research.

"Looking back now, I was rather naïve about business. I had been increasingly involved with my parents' business as they grew older and I took on more responsibility for running things. However, that always just felt like we were teaching drama rather than running a business and there was never a feeling of being part of a business."

Joining P&F and introducing computers

"My husband's company was an export packing and freight forwarding firm. As a packing company it specialised in manufacturing wooden cases and crates for high value products that would be shipped all over the world. At that time, that sort of business was a niche industry and it had been very successful for many years. It had grown to occupy substantial premises and employed around twenty people.

"When I first went to work in P&F, the experience of working in organisations was completely new to me. When I reflect on that time I think about the sort of people that worked in the management roles as compared to myself. The thing that was new to me was an intense feeling of having not only to think about myself, but also about what was going on. Also there was the complication that the company was run by my husband. That bit of context is quite relevant to how I think and how I reflect on the experience I gained over that period.

"One of the first things I worked on was to introduce computers. It was just around the time that small businesses were starting to step up and think about how computing could work for them. Being new, of course, nobody knew exactly what it would mean, nobody quite knew how they would use them, whether or not they were relevant. I thought it sounded like an interesting project, something for me to explore, and I went blindly in thinking that what I was doing was just implementing computers.

"I did quite a lot of research on how we might use them and started by bringing the first computer into the office. I wanted to get a sense of what could be done and what we could draw on in terms of IT.

"What happened in reality, though, was that there was a great deal of tension and anxiety. First of all, it was simply a case of not really wanting to do it. When I say not really wanting to get involved in computers, people did come and say that 'they were quite happy to do it' but then there was huge resistance to using computing. It always seemed that it would be perfect, but not for them, not for their department or not for their situation.

"So, I just started by looking at what things I could do and becoming more familiar with this kind of transference of knowledge. I suppose it was, in those days, that the knowledge held in the business was largely tacit and not set down in any formal way. So the question was, how do you then go about capturing that knowledge formally, using computers? There was a knowledge management aspect to it which made absolute sense. There were a lot of the things that people had got little bits of knowledge about, so why wouldn't you put that into a system that everybody could use?

"I thought we could just move from one way of working to the other. However, what I found was that the tensions played out in quite a personal way towards me. We had one person who just called computers 'Japanese junk'. As the finance director, he kept the company's financial records. He wrote the most beautiful ledgers by hand using turquoise ink. To me it was quite easy to see that all the figures that he was adding up at the end of the month would fit perfectly on to a spreadsheet. In retrospect, I see that a change such as that was going to eat away at his whole identity within the organisation. He put a lot of time in to these hand-written processes and had a lot of animosity towards replacing them with computing. He was convinced that he could do anything the computer could do and he could do it quicker and more efficiently.

"So I arranged to do a comparison. We took a set of figures and put them into a spreadsheet with totals at the bottom and it worked fine. He did the same exercise manually. When he had finished he claimed that the computer had come to the wrong answer, as his figures were different. But of course, when we compared the two sets of figures, those that we were getting from the computer were figures calculated to a number of decimal points, whilst his calculations were rounded. He did accept that the computer had come up with a more accurate calculation but his innate resistance remained. On one level it seemed so trivial, but on the other you can see the anxiety and the lengths that people will go to protect their own bit of the world and to resist change.

"At the time, I just did not understand what this was about. It felt very personal with my husband known in the company, and I felt in a very difficult position in terms of how I might respond. Paul had loyalty both to his staff and to me, which meant that he was also in a really difficult situation. At the simplest level, it sounds like a straightforward thing. You buy a computer, you transfer knowledge, you move from the present way of working to a better, more efficient way. What came as such a surprise to me was a number of tensions that came out of that."

Talking but not communicating

"Something that occurred to me, and this fits into the thing about introducing computers, was that the company was not very good at finding spaces to talk about possible changes and new ways of working. I could see, as an outsider, that it would be useful to address some of these problems. People were always talking about problems and always coming to me with problems but they were much less keen to actually address them. There were patterns of conversations that would recur on a regular basis but there was no willingness to think about it and say: 'Well if this is the problem what might we do about it?'

"In terms of the nature of the packaging and freighting industry there was a lot of shifting in the sort of clients we were working with. The changes coming from globalisation, with lots of manufacturers moving from the UK, impacted on us significantly. Yet that was never really addressed as something that we would want to discuss. There was a huge amount of tension, frustration and anger that people were no longer using our services but there was wasn't a willingness or an openness to think about how we might deal with those issues. How we might create some sort of space for a reflection. A forum where you would engage in an open conversation to explore the problem.

"My experience of change, first of all implementing change in terms of computers but then in the broader view of things, was that there was very little thinking and reflecting on what we are doing together, asking questions such as 'How is this changing for us?' and 'What's happening in the outside world that we need to respond to?'

"So, whilst I tried to have more of those conversations, it was very challenging. I think it was partly because nobody really knew where the industry was going. But there was also a sense of 'If the future is uncertain, then what's the point in talking about it?' and 'Better that we just carry on doing the things where our experience lies, stay with the way things are.'

"It was more than just that we were in a changing environment in terms of technology and the way things were being moved around the world. We were actually packing and shipping, sometimes, very large machinery and specialist items and, of course, what happened was that a lot of those companies were no longer in existence. So the nature of our client base was changing. The profitability of the jobs was changing as things became far more competitive in a shrinking market. With the stripping-out of many of our original customers it became much more competitive. Competitors were now willing to come in and do jobs much more cheaply, under-pricing us. That was very frustrating and annoying, but rather than stopping and thinking 'OK so how are we going to address this? What else could we be doing? How could we think about doing things differently?', we found that having those sorts of conversations about possible change was very difficult."

Making changes

"There was a lot of conflict avoidance going on. It might just be my own perceptions coming in because I was quite new but it definitely felt that the concept of change was quite challenging to everyone. The idea of addressing things face-on and getting things to happen that were different, it was quite difficult. There was a default reaction of avoidance rather than just standing up and addressing things.

"I think that kind of culture is perhaps partly related to the industry we were in, which was very much a kind of old-style industry. They had been around for twenty-five to thirty years so the ways of working fitted into a very hierarchical-type model with the desire to maintain the status quo.

"I suppose challenging that and thinking about how it might be different was difficult for them to imagine. But for me, because I didn't have that kind of structure, I was just interested in asking the questions and that meant that it actually made me quite unpopular. I found it quite difficult being in that situation. It became quite stressful at times. They didn't attack me directly, not physically, and actually not necessarily openly. Because, of course, with Paul being the founder of the company, it made for an interesting dynamic. The take-up of computers was a real example of that, whereby people initially rejected any opportunity to get involved. However, once people found out that it did make their job easier and quicker they started eventually to accept it.

"The finance director, who used to refer to the 'Japanese junk', retired and once he had gone, there was much more acceptance. People started to think that perhaps these computers were things that we can use. He had been the figurehead of the resistance along with his wife. They worked together and once they had both gone there was a really big shift. Now, thinking back, I can see how those dynamics kept things in place, artificially perhaps.

"So, the take-up of computers did happen. By the end of the change we'd moved over the costings process, we had changed the worksheet to become a job-sheet type of arrangement and computerised the stock-taking. Everybody moved to these models and even on the shop floor they had their own computer and would create their own systems. So, I could see, although it took time and tenacity, eventually people's fear that it might change their jobs dissipated. I don't know exactly what they were afraid of but removing some of their anxiety meant that these changes were taken up.

"Ultimately, the introduction of computers did prove to make the business administration more efficient and provide the sort of management information that nowadays businesses take for granted. Nobody lost their job as a direct result of the introduction of the systems, so their anxieties in that respect were unfounded. But the response to the proposal of change was a revelation and I gave a great deal of thought to how subsequent change might be better delivered.

"Following that we certainly had more conversations internally. We had more meetings in an attempt to bring people together to share more information. That was, I think, successful to a point. But having said that, there was still a lot of tension and conflict in individual roles. The people in operations thought that the people in sales weren't doing anything and were offering things to clients that operations couldn't deliver. Even though it was quite a small company, the same tensions that play out in larger organisations were there. I often found myself trying to manage the conflict whilst at the same time trying to think of how we might move forward. That was one of the key challenges for me. How do you overcome these ways of working that are so ingrained in the culture? I found that trying to create the kind of motivation for change just by pointing out the problems doesn't necessarily mean that you are going to get the change. That, for me, was a key bit of learning.

"I had been with the company for about six years, and was gradually getting more and more involved in its management, when Paul decided to retire. He is a few years older than me and was not in good health at the time. So, after having run the business for some twenty-five years he stepped down and I stepped into the role of managing director. There was quite a change, at that time, in the senior management of the company. The finance director and another board director had also retired. So it was a different situation. I felt that I was now in a position to make changes.

"I tried to get people involved and to have a feeling of being listened to. One thing I found interesting was the change in attitudes towards the people on the shop floor. There had always been a perception amongst the staff that the shop floor workers were always whingeing and moaning. By creating opportunities for those workers to talk about the things that worried them shifted those conversations. As a result, they didn't come to me unless there really was a problem. That I saw as a positive.

"We shifted to having more regular meetings and I certainly tried to get people involved. However, and maybe it was my inexperience in thinking about how could we do things differently and because of the industry we were in, there wasn't much opportunity for innovation. It was a very old-fashioned kind of process and it was very difficult, for me, to see how things could be done differently. I had hoped that people within the organisation would want to create some sort of strategic thinking space. But, in terms of coming up with a great solution as to how we might suddenly jump-start ourselves into increasing turnover there was very little consideration of how we might do that."

Failing to confront change

"The turnover of the business was reasonably stable, it wasn't falling hugely but profitability generally was. Because of the general tightening of the economy at the time and the fact that we were the last stage in a logistic journey, everybody was cutting costs and wanting us to do something for less. The company itself was functional. What it was good at doing was what it had always done. However, it wasn't very good at thinking about what it could do differently, despite having those conversations. I felt that we had a good working relationship, but at the same time I felt we couldn't actually talk to each other and shifting into those dialogues about change was tremendously difficult.

"In the end, it was not this lack of conversation about change that brought us to the point of closure. There was certainly a feeling of working well together and that wasn't the reason that we made the decision to close down the company. But the challenge that brought that about, in the end, was a particular shipment. It was a contract for a trusted supplier who had always done work with us. They made a wrong decision relating to the terms of the shipment and it contradicted the conditions that it was supposed to comply with. The lengthy delays that this caused to the shipment, the resulting costs and loss of revenue put us in an impossible position.

"That was really quite a challenge, and whilst we did have opportunities to think about how we might resolve the problems there were underlying issues that did relate to the previous inability to change. Looking back now, one of the key challenges was that the structure of the organisation was quite top heavy in terms of management. This was something that had developed over the years, so our cost base was high in terms of the premises and the number of staff. So it didn't take much for us to be pushed to the limit of our finances. There was a possibility that if we had closed down the company we could have re-opened on a more cost-effective basis. But when it came to the ultimate decision, I just couldn't see that we could guarantee that it would work and ultimately the responsibility would fall on to me to do that. So it was a hard decision but one that I had to take.

"Fortunately, because we took that decision when we did we were able to close the business in an orderly fashion. Pretty much everybody, and in particular the skilled people on the shop floor, were able to secure alternative employment quite quickly. For me, though, it was for some time a feeling of failure. I had, after all, closed down the business that my husband had founded and built up over so many years, although Paul was very supportive of my decision. Ultimately, I feel that I learnt a great deal from my time with the business and without that experience I would not be in the position that I am now."

So, what did I learn?

"I think the first thing, as I'm reflecting now, is that you should never underestimate that change is not a top-down process. That any sort of top-down initiative to change will be taken up in a number of different ways by the individuals for a whole range of reasons that you cannot possibly anticipate. I suppose you could say that I was a bit of an amateur when it came to managing the change that was necessary to take the business forward. Because I hadn't realised that people wouldn't go: 'Well this is great, let's get computers, great, innovative, let's do something new.' That was my assumption and I just couldn't work out why these people were so anxious and angry and frustrated about the imposition of change. So, from that point of view this understanding that no matter what the rationale for the change and how positive it may potentially be, you can't anticipate how people in their day-to-day jobs will respond to opportunities. That is something that I think is fundamental.

"Secondly, I suppose, throughout this process and at the end of it there was this sense of 'How do you have more open conversations? How do you have conversations where you can explore things rather than blaming?'

"I found myself looking for people outside of the business to talk to. Because it became so frustrating that people were very protective of their own corner of the world. I think there is this question: can you predict what an approach to change is going to look like?

"In this case, bringing computers in seemed a nice little rounded project. But in practice it is difficult to put a boundary around what it is you are going to do, why are you going to do it and how it's going to end up.

"In reality there is no certainty, from a strategy point of view. You have to accept that there is really no way of knowing how things will work out. That the world's changing and we need to make sense of it together. Somehow, we've got to have the courage to face up to the fact that individually we might not have the answer but by talking to each other we may be able to find a way forward. That was something that I really took away from my experience at P&F. The importance of not of just talking to people, having conversations, but having those sorts of challenging, open, that is mind-opening, exploratory conversations in which you don't feel threatened. Where you can talk about things without feeling threatened or anxious.

"I think that if I could have had the benefit of hindsight, I would have changed a lot of things. Having the free conversations up front, in terms of why we might be doing it and how we might do it and how we could get more of a buy-in. In trying to bring about change in P&F, I hadn't seen the benefits of getting other people involved; I thought that everybody would just automatically think it was a good idea."

Moving on

"Having completed the close-down of P&F and after some time spent reflecting on that experience, I was keen move on. However, feeling a little bruised, as well, by what I had been through, I wasn't so keen to take on another management role working in an organisation. So I decided that I could use what I had learnt to help others who might be going through similar issues by setting myself up as an independent business consultant. Coming away from the frustration of trying to manage change made me feel that perhaps other people were experiencing some of the same thing. That perhaps some of my knowledge, my learning from this process, may be of use. I saw this as one of the underpinning benefits of the job that I could perhaps encourage people to have these more open types of conversations that had proved to be so difficult at P&F.

"That was certainly at the heart of my practice. A belief in creating opportunities to think and talk about where you are now, where you want to be and what the challenges are. Thinking about the things that you want to talk about, that you may see as the problems, but perhaps you hadn't wanted to share. I saw that this might be a particular issue in a small business, perhaps, as opposed to a large organisation where you are continuously involved in meetings, where you can be involved in strategy. In small firms and particularly very small firms, you very often don't have anybody you can talk to about it.

"There is of course always the risk that if you started telling people that things were really dire and very worrying, they may be scared off, take their knowledge and leave the company. A risk that people will tend to keep everything back and hold everything in. In practice, I found that giving people the opportunity to talk about some of their anxieties, their concerns or their worries was a revelation, not just to me but to them as well. People would say:

'Well, I've never even thought of it like that!'

"Or:

'I can see that this is something I have to think about and address.'

"So, that was very important to the way I proposed to approach my practice. The idea of focusing on thinking in an open conversation about how we might gain a sense of meaning through this kind of 'what's next' conversation, rather than coming in with a solution."

Being let in

"In having these sort of conversations, I have found that there comes a point where there is a change of understanding. The point where a little of the guard is dropped and the conversation begins to open up and you start to get a glimpse of what the real issues may be that the client is facing. It is a feeling of being let in to their confidence where they feel able to trust you with some piece of personal information that is standing in the way of them moving forward. Something that they wouldn't necessarily want to share with their colleagues but could form the basis of an understanding between us. I liken it to that moment in learning a new dance when it all starts to come together. Up until that point you are sort of doing a dance around each other but not with each other. You are trying to follow the steps and not to tread on your partner's feet whilst staying with the beat. All of a sudden you reach a point of understanding where you can trust each other enough to start actually dancing together. It is the point where the process becomes less mechanical and a shared creativity is able to emerge. Similarly, a level of trust is established in the conversation that allows you to work together and explore issues in a more intimate way.

"I remember a particular client that I worked with a few years ago. He ran a small manufacturing business in the Midlands, a family business established by his grandfather. It was suffering a gradual decline due to lack of modernisation, something that I came to understand was not due to a lack of investment finance but to a deeply held resistance to changing what his father had built up. We met at his home, as he didn't want anybody in the business to know that he was seeking advice, and the conversation started off in the normal way. I introduced myself, telling him a little about my experience in helping businesses like his, and he gave me a potted history of the business. He told me about the difficulties that they were facing, most of which he framed in terms of having trouble coping with the external market changes that he felt he had no control over.

"I felt, though, that we were skating around the problem rather than facing up to the need to change and move with the times. It seemed that he was only really showing any passion for the business when he talked about its family history and the importance of maintaining that. So I thought that perhaps if I dug into that a little further we might be able to open up the conversation and get to the real reason why he, and the business, couldn't move forward. Rather than ask him directly about his family I spoke a little about my own. I talked about my parents' family business, how we had actually all worked together in the business when I was younger and how important that experience had been to me growing up. He listened quietly and there was a long silence when I had finished speaking before he said: 'My mother was taken very ill when I was young and my father struggled to bring up the family and to grow the business. I worked very hard to help my father and to protect him and the family.' I asked him to tell me more about that time and he told me at some length and with considerable emotion about how he had worked alongside his father to secure the business and provide for his family. From that point, I felt that he had let me in to his world and shared his fears and the conversation flowed. I told him of my experiences and he opened up about his feelings of how important the business was to him.

"It became clear to both of us, as the conversation progressed, that his difficulty in modernising the business was not coming from any external issue but from his own protective feelings towards the business and the sense of security that it gave him. The risks in modernisation, as he saw them, were a threat to his sense of security that was embodied by the business as it was. I then was actually able to work with him, over the next year or so, building on that understanding, to find a way for the business to move forward in a way that secured its future whilst maintaining its values.

"I suppose in contrast to that experience, one of the things that I felt, at least with some of the people at P&F, was that I never got to that stage where I felt let in. It would have been great if we had been able to shift to a more open form of conversation."

Learning to dance

"With clients, when you are in an advisory role, you are faced with a situation where they really don't know you. When you are working in a company, you have history, and there are all sorts of tensions playing out, such as, what you are going to say and what you are not going to say. Whereas the difference when you're with a client on a one-to-one basis, that you have never met before, is: how do we get to that point of being let in? You have to be prepared for the fact that it doesn't always happen. The more I work with clients the more I realise how important it is to find a shared understanding and meaning. The point where you recognise in each other some area where you have a shared understanding. This sense of being let in.

"Often when you are at that point it will allow much more personal information and concerns to be aired. That, in itself, can be difficult for the client because they can feel quite vulnerable sharing such things. For the advisor, you then have to think about what you do with this information. How do you work together to make sense of it, and how does that turn into positive change?

"I think that has always been at the heart of it for me, from an advisory point of view. You have a conversation. You explore these things. Together you might come up with some ideas for action and you need to capture those ideas. But would they be taken up? Would they be turned into new ways of working in the business? There was always no way of telling.

"What I find interesting in these interactions is that you never know what is going to emerge. Often, I find that I have said something in these conversations. Something that didn't necessarily resonate at the time but had caused a change to emerge later. Sometime later I would be speaking to somebody else and they would say: 'Oh I met so-and-so and they were saying how helpful what you had said had been.' You are then thinking: 'Well what did I say?'

"I remember one occasion recently where we had one of my clients come to the Business School to do an MBA masterclass. In the midst of the class she suddenly announced: 'Oh yes, Ruth, who is my mentor, told me that one of the problems that I was having with my business was that, when I'm selling, I'm making a complex sale.' I'm then sitting there thinking, 'I don't really recall saying that. When did I say that? Just remind me.' Then I remembered that about four or five years previously, when we were working together, she had been creating the sort of products that people buy more as a gift for somebody else than a personal purchase.

"In our conversation at the time, one of the things that had occurred to me was to wonder who the customer was. Because if the person who receives the gift isn't the person paying for it, how does the person who did pay the money know that it is good value? How do you build a relationship with someone who is receiving the product when they haven't invested their money in it?

"So, this idea of a complex sale was just a way of exploring what this might mean and for her, it hit the spot. Then, four to five years later, that's been the thing that shaped the way that she saw a key issue with her business. You just can't tell what might get taken up or resonate; it's only in the forming of the conversation that things come into awareness and you find in the emerging understanding that you might have some experience to add to it.

"For me, the top-down approach is not what advising is about. You don't go in as an advisor to tell people what to do. Although that is generally what people think you should be doing. It is, perhaps more of an art than a science. A process of mutual exploration to find common ground from where you can begin to make progress. It is not something you can plan. There is no fixed blueprint of how to get to that point of understanding and no defined way of knowing when you have got there.

"It's a visceral feeling. You know when you have been let in and yet you can't control it. You can't make it happen. You can work towards it happening and be part of it. It's kind of that learning to dance thing but even more. It's being ready to respond. It is the kind of, sense of interconnectivity that you can't put a finger on. Some sense of shared understanding.

"I have often found that, in a change situation, people will question your knowledge.

'How come that you are you able to tell me what to do, when you don't know anything about my business?'

'I'm the expert in what I do, so why should I listen to you?'

"In other words: 'I'm not going to let you in, because you do not know my world, and I'm not going to share my world with you.'

"I have been in so many businesses where there has been this sort of attitude of 'What could you do, how could you possibly be of any benefit to my business?'

"My first reaction to that is one of relief because I think, 'Great, well we are at a really good starting point. This person is being honest with me. They actually don't think I'm going to be any use.' I'm starting from the lowest point.

"In these situations, the first thing I do is to show that I will be honest with them. I say: 'Do you know what, it may be that there is nothing I can do; however, I do have quite a lot of experience of everything and if you want to tell me a little about your business then we can just see where this goes.'

"When they start telling you about their business, more often than not they actually start to find things out about themselves and their business, that they hadn't even thought of before. That gives you an opening where you can say 'Well okay, so this sounds to me like this sort of issue ….'

"Then that's the bite. It's a gesture of saying something and getting a response. It is inviting you to then contribute and step into that conversation. It's almost like there is a shared invitation to go on together.

"So, there's this sort of shielding of 'What do you know about my business? I don't think that you can help me at all, I'm not even willing to invest my time and energy into sharing any information with you because this is going to be of no use to me.'

"Then there is a shifting to a point where they're saying 'Well, hang on a minute, yeah, I have got a bit of a worry here and if you can help me with this a little bit we will see where it goes.'

"That's the first step. It may be that you suggest something and they will shut you down with 'Yeah, well, that will never work anyway.'

"But very often it's:

'OK, well I'm going to invite you to think about this a little bit and depending on your response I may consider sharing some more. But I'm not going to do that until such time as I feel comfortable and confident that the energy I'm putting into communicating with you has some benefit to me.'

"As an advisor, on the other hand, of course, you are being paid to go and have that conversation. So you are thinking about what can you do with this piece of information. It is very much like the dance. You are a partner in the process rather than a detached, objective, director of proceedings. You are engaged in a process and once you have accepted that there is some shared benefit, then you can just see where it goes. It can take some time to do that. To explore what each person is willing to commit to in terms of sharing information in that conversation. It's a process of gauging the willingness to engage in an ongoing conversation within that response. It is in a sense a process of trial and error. But it's also a gut feeling. It's like:

'OK so I've tried this and they responded that way. So, that looks as though they might be interested in that rather than this.'

"I find it fascinating how, through this sort of approach, the change that is really needed to move a business forward seems to emerge in this sort of conversation rather than a more formal prescriptive approach. It sort of mirrors how my own progress has evolved. As I said, I never set out to become a business manager or indeed a business advisor, helping others to change. However, over time I became more and more interested in understanding what was actually happening in these situations, and that has led me into academia. I am still engaged with my advisory business but I now also lecture and do management research at the Business School."

Challenging perceptions

"These two worlds recently came together when I went to do a workshop for some women in business. It followed a similar session about leading in a business and planning strategy.

"In that first session, I felt we had had some really interesting conversations, but I just got this feeling that it hadn't got to the point where we had really shifted, in some sense, to a new understanding. It felt almost laboured, in a way that it had, sort of, served its purpose but there was something missing. Something that would have taken it to a higher level. I had some theoretical models and I thought about how we might engage differently in the next session. But it always stuck in my mind that there was something about it that lacked flow.

"So, in trying to get my head around this, I started to think about the various situations I had experienced both in P&F and when working with individual clients as an advisor. My first thought was that at P&F I was part of the business, I was part of that community trying to bring about change. Then second, I thought, when I was working as an advisor with a client it was very often very intimate. In that setting, it is just me and the client. Somebody who doesn't really know me. In each case, to be able to move forward, in a way that is truly innovative, there needs to be a building of trust, a mutual 'letting-in' by the participants.

"In P&F we all knew each other and we had a shared history. But when you are with a client it's only one-to-one, or one-to-two at most, which is a very different dynamic in terms of being able to respond to them and build a relationship. When you're working with a group of people who are all from different companies, as was the case in the workshop, there is yet another dynamic. They don't really know each other and the whole trust thing has to be built in the same way as working with a new client. You have to build trust on a one-to-one basis within a group environment. As a facilitator, how you build, manage, maintain and sustain the relationships when they are in a group is very different. This was a situation that I felt less comfortable with. This was playing on my mind as I did the second session a few weeks later and I thought there must be a different way of doing this.

"So, this second session was all about business planning for small businesses. How they might think about their strategy and bring about change. There were about ten or twelve in the group. But, rather than coming in with 'We are going to do a bit about an action plan and this is what strategy and change is about,' I started off by saying 'OK, I'm going to give you one minute to just write down everything that is good about your business. Anything you think of – you don't have to share it with anyone but just write for a minute.'

"So they did that and it was very interesting. They were engaged with the process and there was a whole lot of energy in the room with everybody scribbling away. Then after the minute was up I said 'OK, you've done that now you are going to have a further minute to write on one issue or any problem, anything you've wanted to capture.'

"I left them to do that for a minute, then I said 'You don't have to say anything, but is there anything people would like to share?'

"So someone immediately put a hand up and said 'Actually, can I just say, I can't believe what happened then. Because, I went to write something but what I actually wrote was something completely different.'

"I asked her: 'Are you willing to share it?'

"She replied: 'Yes, I am, I was going to write what was good about my business but actually what I found myself writing was "Having a small business makes me feel valued as an individual. It's important to me. For me it's important, something that's important for me to do. I had never thought about it before and that's really different for me."'

"So, suddenly, whilst it felt a bit scary, we were opening up a completely different conversation.

"Then somebody two seats away from the first person, said 'Actually, can I just say, now you have said that, what I wrote is that for me my business is so important because I've had so many years of doing things for everybody else and this is the first time that I'm doing something for me.' Then she burst into tears.

"Well that's a little bit tricky, but I'm thinking this is so much more authentic.

"Then a third person said: 'The thing that I have written is that people keep telling me I've got to plan and I don't want to. Why should I make a plan? But now I've started thinking, this isn't about writing a plan this about writing something for me. It's about what I want to do in my business. It's not about writing a plan that's out there.'

"I found that we had started a process in which we had created a perfectly different environment. One in which we could then say 'Well, there is no such thing as the perfect plan and the perfect action plan for you. You've got to start where you are and think about what is important to you. So that you can actually start writing plans that are relevant.'

"I realised then that what had happened, and linking that into change, was exactly the opposite of the top-down approach. As a facilitator, it made me realise that it takes courage to stay with the uncertainty and when somebody starts crying in that group situation, then you have really got them to open up. For people to be able to say, in that sort of forum, that 'my business matters' is a realisation that they are, of course, emotionally involved in it.

"To think that we can imagine that isn't happening is to deny the actual nature of organisations. For a change manager or business leader, you can see it is a lot easier to hide behind a model or framework. To just tell people 'Here is a model, fill it in and the job's done.'

"In terms of how I felt about that session, when I came away I just thought that for me it was so much more than teaching at people. It was getting people to engage in where they are, personally, in the process. We were working together openly and taking their ideas forward.

"The problem is, when I am thinking about change and I put myself back in the P&F situation, I believe that if I had the courage, the skills and the understanding that I now have it may have turned out differently. It's still not easy, but maybe by shifting to these more responsive ways I could have been able to just say:

'Look, wouldn't we be better off doing it together?'

'What are you most worried about?'

'What do you think is going on and what can we do about it?'

'What are your biggest concerns?'

"Being able to stay with that, maybe things would have been different.

"I just felt that, when it really came down to the choice of being able to keep the company going or not, I just couldn't see then that it was something that I could sustain over time. But by actually being able to stay with it, to encourage people to be open and honest with their feelings about change and work through that, it's got to be a better way than inflicting people with change and believing that somehow, they will come on board and just accept a new reality. When in fact that reality is constantly being constructed and reconstructed by everybody in different ways. So it isn't possible to predetermine the future when the reality of those involved in any change is constantly changing and often completely hidden from our understanding."

Thoughts on Ruth's story

What makes Ruth's story illuminating is the fact that she came to managing change in P&F, as, in her words, an amateur. Consequently, she takes a view of organisations and the behaviour of those she was working with as they actually were. She soon discovered that people react to change in unpredictable and often counter-intuitive ways. Her work as an advisor revealed the extent to which such reactions are driven by the deeply held values and beliefs of our personal unconscious realities.

Ruth's description of being let in to a more open and personal level of conversation with her clients, points to the emergence of new ways of thinking where the relationship moves towards the 'edge of chaos', through the strengthening of the connection between them. In the same way that Jim was able to move forward by bringing his unconscious reality into his conscious thought, Ruth describes how facing that challenge can move thinking to a new place. In P&F the failure to do that ultimately contributed to the closure of the company. However, in her business planning workshop, challenging the small business leaders to reveal their personal feelings allowed them to think differently about what they expected from the process.

Reflecting on her experience of change as a manager, business advisor and latterly an academic has prompted Ruth to challenge the conventional view of a top-down, planned and managed approach to change, and move to that of a process arising from personal, self-challenging, interactive conversation.

In the next chapter, we will explore how people come to make the choice to change. To move to an uncertain and emergent future.

5 Choosing to change in the face of the unknown

In Jim's story of change in Chapter 1, we saw how he changed in a way that was entirely unpredictable at the start of the programme. Whilst the improvement of management skills was one of the objectives and, as he says, the training provided him with some skills that he later applied, the way that his life changed was a surprise to him and emerged from his choice to take a new approach to his future. The experience of exploring his deeply held beliefs about himself in the one-to-one session that he describes, allowed him to reform his unconscious reality. Resolving issues held in his implicit attitude by choosing to confront them explicitly, enabled him to move forward.

Ruth's story tells of how people seek to protect their own 'corner of the world', acting in seemingly irrational ways to justify their views. Her narrative speaks of the sense of 'being let in' at the point of choice where they are open to facing the challenge of change.

In this chapter, we look at how we make choices and the challenge of taking a step into the unknown.

As we move through life we are constantly making choices: choices about how to act – should I do this or do that? How to behave – to politely pass or argue the point; or which path to take – do I take the job or look for something better? We may think that these choices are considered, thoroughly thought through and deliberate, but as we have seen in Chapter 3, they are generally unconscious decisions, choices driven by past experience hardwired into our unconscious reality.

As life unfolds we are faced by a continually changing environment and experience that we have no direct control over. The choices that we make are set in the context of all the choices made by others, from which the unexpected will tend to emerge. In an organisational setting, deliberate change programmes which will, by definition, be intended to have the best of positive effects are set into an ongoing background of change. We cannot isolate the organisation or a specific intended change process from that background. The choices being made by those involved in respect of that change will be unavoidably affected by their present experience of all the change going on in their lives.

The story of Ruth's attempts to introduce computers into P&F shows how people can react. Their use would on the face of it both then and now, with considerable hindsight, seem to be obviously beneficial. However, the reaction was at best unenthusiastic and at worst actively resisted. There was an ongoing cultural, economic and technological background to the change which is still ongoing. The increasing use of desktop computers in business was just a step along the road that had started with the postwar development of computing power. The transfer of that power into individual machines that could be used in the office and home together with software such as spreadsheets, designed for business, has brought computers into common use. Twenty-five years on, the use of computers and the access to knowledge through the internet that they bring is indispensable.

Nowadays, how we should use social media in organisations carries similar arguments and resistance from some, as we hear in this narrative. The resistance that Ruth encountered was driven by two deeply held emotions. First, the finance director's feelings of being threatened by what he saw as his replacement by the computer. Then second, the general resistance to having to learn something new, expressed by staff saying that they saw a potential benefit but it was not for them or their department. In both cases the logic of using computers was not the issue, at least for the finance director once the accuracy of a spreadsheet had been demonstrated. The resistance was driven by their adherence to a personal reality that did not accept the utility of computers, a reality that had been constructed in a world that did not include computers; and they were not ready to make the choice to change.

Faced with the need for organisational change we are required to make choices. Do we accept or reject the change? Do we accept part of it and reject the rest? Do we resist the change or work to change it to our preference? In any choice made there is an element of risk assessment involved. In everyday life, the assessment of risk is an ongoing and largely unconscious activity. When crossing a road, the assessment is obvious. Is traffic approaching? How fast is it approaching? What is the likelihood of the driver changing speed or direction? Is there anything to prevent you crossing quickly and achieving your desired outcome? All these and many other factors are weighed up instantaneously in the decision whether to cross at that point and time. Our propensity to take risk is weighed by our experience. Where we have taken risks in the past and suffered the consequences, our reality will reflect that and we will unconsciously tend to avoid that outcome in the present. We may take time to make a conscious assessment considering all the possible outcomes and the chances of their happening. But how we act in the present will still be a choice made in the present driven by our unconscious reality. The successful implementation of prescribed change in an organisational setting, then, is dependent on the individuals connected with the change making a choice to reform their reality, to accept and work with that change.

In Chapter 3 we considered the alternative view of change based on complexity theory and looked at the work of Stuart Kauffman on complex adaptive systems. His work also looked at the concept of fitness landscapes and how the behaviour of systems operating at the 'edge of chaos' might be able to move across such landscapes, thus avoiding the trap of incremental improvement that prevents innovation. We now look at how these ideas can inform our thinking about change and how we may make a choice to change.

Fitness landscapes

The concept of fitness derives from Darwin's evolutionary model and the survival of the fittest. In this context, the species or the individual within that species that is best suited to survive is the one that is most able to adapt to its changing environment. The species that is best able to reproduce and maintain its future. So, the fitness criteria will include the ability to find sufficient food whilst avoiding being taken as food by others; the ability to find shelter or resist the elements; the ability to breed and provide nourishment for its young. The fittest species, in order to fulfil its objective of survival, has to be able to change as its environment changes.

We can imagine the level of fitness of a species, as represented by its position on an undulating landscape, a simulation of a natural landscape of hills, mountains and valleys where the higher you are above sea level the higher level of fitness you have.

The fitness of a system, or an agent in a system is, as we have defined above, dependent on the strength of several related factors. If we model those as dimensions we have a space which represents the strength of all the possible combinations of those criteria. In terms of species survival, one dimension may represent the ability to catch prey and another the ability to avoid being preyed upon. If the level of fitness – the chance of survival given by the combination of these criteria – is represented by the height above a common plane then we have a fitness landscape. On such a landscape, survival is most likely for those species which occupy the highest positions. The topography of the landscape is emergent from the complex system of competing factors of survival. Your position on the landscape, on the top of the mountain or at the bottom of the valley, determines your chances.

As with a natural mountainous landscape the topography will change over time. Mountain peaks will be pushed up by the changing pressure in the ground and the movement of the land masses. At the same time those same peaks are being worn down by the elements eroding the uplands and building up the valleys. Thus, the landscape is shaped by multi-dimensional factors.

It may be easier to think of multi-dimensional influences by an analogy with the surface of the ocean. A complex set of factors combine to shape the surface of the sea at any time. The prevailing air pressure above the surface, the relative difference between the temperature of the air and the water, the varying depth of water, ocean currents and the gravitational pull of the moon are all factors. Together they create at any one time a surface seascape that changes continually between flat calm and mountainous waves. The environment occupied by an organisation is similarly shaped by complex and interrelated factors such as the level of economic activity, interest rates, tax levels, public opinion and brand loyalty, trade policies and political opinion. The result is an ever-changing business and social environment where organisations must constantly strive to improve to survive. The analogy of such an environment as a landscape that organisations, within a changing environment, must ascend to improve their fitness, is a powerful one.

An organisation that improves its level of fitness will climb up the landscape to a higher position. Using again, the example of species survival, a hunting animal may improve its ability to catch prey and move up the slope along that dimension by increasing its swiftness in the chase. That dimension of success is, though, relative to the susceptibility of its prey to being caught by speed alone. Development, by the preyed upon species, of the ability to swim, to avoid capture by taking to the water, would make additional speed redundant. In this way, the landscape for this species has changed and it will need to find alternative ways to enhance its fitness. The number of criteria involved determines the contours of a fitness landscape in a complex system. The more complex the systems, the more rugged the landscape, with increasing numbers of peaks representing different solutions to fitness. As interrelated systems change and the fitness of the interacting individuals changes, the contours of each system's landscape will change.

The story of P&F's struggle for survival and its difficult position between competing organisations in the global business environment is an example of a changing landscape. The normal response of change managers is to apply various programmes to improve the performance of organisations. Lean management campaigns to reduce wastage and process re-engineering to eliminate unnecessary activity are carried out to improve efficiency. Organisations restructure regularly to keep costs down and take advantage of changing markets. Systems are introduced to improve product and service quality. But all the while they are doing that the landscape of their business environment around them is changing. Their competitors are making similar improvements, markets are changing and demand for their products or services may be declining despite their better quality. The typical efficiency improvement programmes like lean management and quality management take incremental steps up a single dimension, climbing a particular fitness peak. If the programme is successful, the company will move up the fitness peak to be closer to the summit, and if that was the summit of the only peak on the landscape, it would then be one of the fittest in its environment.

However, in a complex world the fitness landscape is extremely rugged. There will be a very large number of peaks and finding the optimal fitness position will be very difficult. A process of logical incrementalism, or linear thinking, will be of little use in finding the highest position. If you have ever been hill walking you will be familiar with the fact that as you ascend one peak there is always a higher peak coming into view, one that cannot be reached by climbing further, only by retreating and taking a different route. So, incremental progress of this sort will very soon lead one to the top of a local peak unable to move laterally to explore other possibly higher peaks by the very process of improvement.

The alternative to the incremental process is to search the entire landscape, testing each position to find the highest. This would, in any rugged landscape, be an extremely lengthy process. The chances of finding the optimum fitness position would be very low. Stuart Kauffman (1995: 248), in his work on organisations, suggests that organisations will never find the optimum fitness position in their ever-changing landscapes. The best they can hope for is to search out the excellent peaks and track them as the landscape reforms. He observes that a natural process of patching appears to be one way that complex systems and organisations optimise this search process.

Using patching to strengthen connectivity

Patching is the process that has, throughout evolution, provided the means by which organisms and ultimately individuals have been able to find novel patterns of behaviour. Rather than being managed, it is an instinctive and emergent process enabling networks to remain close to the 'edge of chaos', able to traverse the fitness landscape and improve their chances of survival.

We saw in Chapter 3 how a complex adaptive system that is operating at, or close to, the 'edge of chaos' will tend to produce new and innovative patterns. That is the transitional condition where the level of connectivity is high but not too high and the number of individuals acting in the network is high but not too high – the level where these two variables combine to produce ever-changing creative, novel but recognisable patterns of behaviour. In an organisational context we can look on these as being new ways of thinking, behaving or working that could have the potential to move the business to a higher point on the fitness landscape.

New organisations, particularly those developing a new product or service, seldom start fully formed; that is, complete with separate departments for their specialist functions such as accounts or human resources. They tend to start off with a small group of people who have a particular interest or an idea for a new product. The stories of the growth of the global IT companies are typical of this form of startup company where a few individuals get together to work on an idea.

In those early days, there tends not to be any formal structure. Without any formal division of labour those involved will share whatever is required to get the company going, develop the product, do the marketing, invoice the customers and submit the accounts. As a small group, they will act as a single network with a common objective of delivering the product and growing the company. They will be working closely together and connections between them will be strong, holding them close to the 'edge of chaos' and enabling them to find novel solutions to growth. However, for the organisation to continue to grow in this way it needs to maintain that position at the 'edge of chaos'. That is where the process of patching develops.

As the organisation grows and more people become involved, individuals tend to focus on the activities where they are most skilled and specialists are brought in to manage particular aspects of the business. As the network grows in this way the number of connections increases and the patterns tend to move beyond the 'edge of chaos' towards unstable and unsustainable behaviour. The ability to continue finding new solutions will be diminished unless the business can find a way to move back towards the 'edge of chaos' position.

It is at this point where the structure starts to emerge. The organisation will start to divide into specialist areas based on the skill sets of the individuals and the demands placed upon it by its environment, for example the need to submit tax returns. Whilst all the people in the organisation share the same overall objectives of growth and profitability, local objectives begin to form within the specialist groups. Those in the accounts department will be concerned with balancing the books and complying with standards and regulations. Those in the research and development group will be focused on producing the best possible product and staying ahead of the competition.

The objective of the different departments or groups may not be compatible. The accountants' focus on maximising annual profit may conflict with the research group's demand for money to invest in product development. In this way, the connections across the boundaries between the groups are weakened. The members of one group may, in the pursuit of their local objective, act in ways that are detrimental to another. The overspend on research and development could result in an improved product but at the same time cause a worsening of the profit margin for the accountants.

In this way, the organisation has evolved into the set of patches, represented by the various groups or departments. The networks within each patch are able to remain at the 'edge of chaos' by reducing the number of individuals and strengthening their connections by sharing local objectives. At the same time, the patches created by the groups have formed a network of their own connected across their boundaries by the interaction between the departments and pursuing the overall company objectives.

As the company continues to grow, further groups will be formed as the need to focus on specialist areas increases. Newly formed departmental patches will sub-divide into teams, such as the Human Resources Department setting up groups to deal with recruitment and employee relations. Each division has the effect of strengthening connectivity in the groups and the overall organisation, keeping them close to the 'edge of chaos'.

We can see the parallel here with biology and evolution in the growth of the foetus in the womb from a single cell to a connected network of specialist organs sustaining life. Similarly, as civilisation has evolved, we have moved from individual self-sufficiency to specialisation as doctors, lawyers, postal workers and politicians. It is in this way that all complex systems are able to maintain a position at the 'edge of chaos' where novel, fitter solutions can emerge.

We can best illustrate patching by an example that will be familiar to most people. By considering football's Premier League as a patched, complex, adaptive system, we can see how each of the twenty component teams is a patch in that system. As a whole, the Premier League is a network of individuals, each of whom have their own personal objectives in their careers in football and are governed in that endeavour by their individual personal schema. Those schemas are composites of the rules of the game, the codes of conduct and the particular disciplines of their job. They are all connected and interact with each other through their common interest in the game, organisations such as the Professional Footballers' Association, the sports media and the Premier League itself. Each individual will bring his or her own values and personal characteristics to the way in which they interact with the other players and people in the system.

The overall network has an objective to achieve the highest standards in football through competition. Individuals within the network will have personal objectives of being, for example, recognised as the best player in the league or the highest goal scorer. If the system was to operate solely as a single network, i.e. without any team loyalty or objectives to be the top team and with every player simply pursuing their personal objectives, then the number of connections between all the individual players and all those that they interact with would be very high. The system would tend towards chaotic behaviour. The pursuit of solely individual objectives within the competition could lead, at best, to some rather selfish forms of play. Consequently, the sport has evolved over the years into a patched network of teams, leagues and national sides.

Let us focus on the UK Premier League, which as we know is divided into teams. Each team shares the overall objective of the league through its membership. The objective of each team within the league, however, is to outplay all the others and end the season at the top of the league. Achievement of one team's objectives in a match will, by the rules of the league, be detrimental to the other team's objective. The loyalty of the players to their team and its success in the league competition means that their professional connections with players in other teams is weakened in favour of those with their fellow team members. Each team, in common with the individuals, has the ability to reflect on their achievements as the season progresses, making changes to tactics and managers accordingly, to pursue their objectives.

All those who gamble on the results of football matches each week will testify to the unpredictability of the outcome of each interaction. The order of the teams in the table and the winning team at the end of the season is emergent from the interactions of the teams over the course of the season. The teams in the league are acting as patches in the complex adaptive system which is the Premier League. The team structure allows each team to seek a position of greater fitness to win matches by working close to the 'edge of chaos'.

In describing connectivity, we used an example of a system of light bulbs. The pattern of 'on' and 'off' which is reached by the system is determined by the connectivity of the system and its sensitivity. This is related to the number of connections and the probability of reaction between the bulbs. That level of connectivity will determine whether the system will either be stable, frozen in a single state, repeating a short sequence of patterns, or completely chaotic. If we could imagine that such a system was adaptive then the effects of a change in the status of one bulb and the resultant change in the overall pattern will be measured against the system's overall objective. The objective, in this example, could be to reach the highest possible number of lit bulbs in the system. As an adaptive system, it can move towards its objective. When a system is acting as a single patch then the level of connectivity at which the system switches between stable and chaotic will be lower relative to the total number of agents or in this case, bulbs.

In a patched network, the overall connectivity of the system remains the same but the assessment of progress against the objective, in response to changes in the status of any of the bulbs, is made within that patch. So, in this way, each patch becomes a sub-system of the original and progress is measured locally. A change in one patch may adversely affect the progress of a neighbour. A change in the status of a bulb on the boundary may prompt a reaction in a bulb on the boundary of an adjacent patch that is connected across the boundary.

This reaction may, in turn, spark a new pattern within that adjacent patch. The assessment of that change will be measured against the objective of that patch only. The dynamic of this arrangement is to create a new network in which the agents are all the patches in the overall network. The patches themselves now constitute the agents in the overall network and are connected by the interactions across the boundaries. The sum of the individual connections across each boundary constitutes the interaction between the separate patches.

The interactions between the patches are feedback relationships that are constantly changing. They are collectively non-linear, with a low probability of certainty, due to the complex nature of the interaction that involves all the switch connections along the boundary. Like each team in the Premier League, each patch will assess progress at each step in time, against its particular objective. As a complex adaptive system, the group of patches, like the teams that make up the Premier League, will produce self-organising emergent patterns that will tend to move towards the overall objective. One team will emerge as league champions.

The evolution of the game of football by this process of patching has enabled it to continually change in response to its emerging environment over the years. New patterns of behaviour have emerged, rules have been changed and the structure of the patches, i.e. the leagues and the teams, has changed. Whilst new patterns have emerged they remain recognisable, as we would expect of behaviour close to the 'edge of chaos'. Throughout the development of the game, as the old newsreels show, from the local sporting rivalry to a global multi-million-pound business and world competitions, it is still recognisable for what it is, the game of football.

In an organisational context, each department will pursue its own objectives, sometimes to the detriment of other departments, and as a complex system the network of departments will pursue the overall company objective. In wider society, self-interest groups will pursue their own objectives and, generally, those groups will interact to achieve the wider objectives. In that way organisations and society evolve to higher levels of fitness.

The tendency to sub-divide is the natural response of complex systems to maintain their behaviour close to the 'edge of chaos'. The increase in the number of patches causes the system to move to a higher level of connectivity before reaching the critical point between stability and instability. This allows a higher number of agents within the overall system to be maintained within the stable zone.

Dividing the system into too many patches, however, will move the system to the unstable condition. So, an optimal situation is to divide the system such that stability is maintained for a larger overall number of agents while not producing instability. Division is required so that the variety of possible patterns is increased whilst the system is maintained close enough to stability for the patterns to be settled and recognisable. The system, therefore, is optimal when it operates close to, but just on the stable side of the 'edge of chaos'. The result of the division of the system in this way, in pursuit of the common objective, is a higher level of emergence of patterns within a higher level of stability.

Patching in organisational and social contexts

Introducing the concept of patching to a complex system increases the number of possibilities open to that system in developing different solutions in pursuit of an objective. The range or diversity of the solutions is increased. Connectivity across the boundaries, whilst isolating the patches in their reactions to those connections, allows a situation where the fitness of one patch can be temporarily reduced by the change in status of a boundary agent in a neighbouring patch. The effect is to cause that affected patch to move down the fitness landscape rather than up. As the diversity of solutions that are possible is increased by the system moving towards the 'edge of chaos', so the bigger the backward step possible becomes, allowing the system to move from peak to peak in single jumps. So, moving systems towards, and maintaining them, at the 'edge of chaos' provides a way for the organisation to access the diversity of higher peaks on their fitness landscape.

In Jim's story in Chapter 1, we can see an example of a patched network. The depot structure of the business that developed as the company grew and spread its customer base across the country, has created a set of patches. Whilst all the individuals share the objectives of the overall business, each of them has a local focus on the success of their particular location. Jim describes how his staff at the Southeast Depot found a new way to work together and were energised to achieve improved performance against the

KPIs set by the change programme. The strengthening of connections between the staff arising from the improved communication, particularly in the one-to-ones and bringing the technicians directly into those conversations, moved them towards the 'edge of chaos'. A new approach to working together emerged and the atmosphere changed. In Jim's words, 'By this time, we were absolutely flying. We were getting good results. The negative stuff wasn't there anymore.'

At the same time, the change programme had introduced weekly tele-conferences, providing a communication channel between the depots that hadn't existed previously. The patches represented by the depots were effectively joined together to form a network of their own. Jim describes how:

> They [the staff in his depot] came to see in the weekly results and in the teleconferences, how they were doing in comparison with the other depots on the programme. A fact that spurred them on, not wanting to be the ones called to account on the call.

The connections between individuals in the various depots were strengthened by the conference calls and personal interactions. The operations manager, senior managers and the consultants on the programme working across the depots further strengthened the connections between the patches. The things that worked well and those that didn't were communicated across the boundaries. As a whole, the network of patches that made up the company's depots was moved towards the 'edge of chaos' and new patterns of working emerged. Jim points to this in the ongoing changes in the way they measure performance and collect data: 'further improvements have meant that we are much better organised'.

With the growth of the internet and the advent of social media there is a growing focus by people on the number of connections or friends they have. Celebrity is measured by the number of followers a person has, professional status by the number of connections made. The internet has made it possible to communicate with an ever-increasing number of people. Messages and responses conveying information, and often misinformation, can be shared in a matter of seconds across the world. Unfortunately, the volume of com-munication is not necessarily an indicator of its quality. We can, in modern times, have any number of connections; however, the degree of connectivity will vary greatly. There is only a small number of people that we will have a very close connection with. Immediate family, long-term friends or close colleagues are the sorts of people with whom we may have a deep under-standing of each other, where we feel each other's emotions and know how they will react.

Beyond them there is a group of friends or relations that we have less of a connection with, those with whom we share a common interest, maybe socially or professionally. Then there are the people we see occasionally, maybe on an ad-hoc basis, in the community. Finally, there are all the 'friends' on social media that we exchange messages with but don't really know. Of course, all the connections you have cannot be neatly placed into categories like this. The point is though, that we have a wide variation in the level of connection that we have with each other and the degree of understanding that exists between us.

We know from contemporary neurological research that the degree of unconscious connection between individuals is far greater than we have previously appreciated. However, that is limited to interpersonal interaction, and again the span of connection is varied and often limited to a smaller number of people than we might think. This naturally limited span of connection forms groups, or patches, within society and organisations within and across the formal division of departmental structure and social groupings. These patches are constantly forming and reforming. Relationships are formed, lost and re-formed. The strength and depth of understanding changes over time whilst the connections across the boundaries of the patches are maintained by the weaker and wider connections across the overall networks.

The emergence of patches in an organisational setting tends to regulate the number of individuals in each network, keeping the number of connections high but not too high, moving the system towards the 'edge of chaos'. At the same time, the strengthening of connections also tends to move it towards the 'edge of chaos' and the forming of novel patterns. The strength of connection, in this context, relates to the degree of influence of one person in the network to bring about change in another. The constant forming and reforming in relationships tends to strengthen connections between individuals, and together with the fluid nature of the patching that goes with that, will tend to move the networks overall towards the 'edge of chaos'. In this way, we are able to create multiple solutions and challenge individuals, organisations and society to move across a fitness landscape and evolve to higher peaks.

If, though, connections are weakened, the system will tend to move away from the 'edge of chaos' to a more stable state where patterns of behaviour are endlessly repeated. Ultimately, the system will settle on a single state and remain unchanged.

We saw in P&F Ltd how the unwillingness of staff to discuss the challenges that they were facing meant that they were unable to change. The view expressed that 'If the future is uncertain then what is the point of looking at it?' and that they should just keep on doing what they knew best, weakened the connections between them in terms of addressing the issues. They became trapped in a repeated pattern of having the same conversations and failing to open up to the challenge of globalisation that they were facing. In the end it was this inability to make the choice to change, to have the difficult conversations that would challenge their perceptions and unconscious feelings about the organisation, that made the future of the company unsustainable. As the level of connectivity reduced, both between individuals and departments, patterns of behaviour became more stable. The ability to innovate and change was stifled.

It is making the choice to change and face up to the difficult truths that challenge one's unconscious reality, that makes real change so hard to accomplish.

Novel patterns and innovation

Through Herbert Mead's description of communication between individuals, by a process of gesture and response and the understanding of complex responsive processes, developed by Ralph Stacey and his colleagues, we can appreciate the nature of human interaction. In organisations that interaction is through language. Despite the rise of the email and various forms of social media, conversations are the primary form of communication and the way in which collective decisions are made. Using our analogy of complex adaptive systems, we know that, as the strength of the connection between individuals increases, the patterns emerging move from being stable and repetitive, through the novel self-organisation state at the 'edge of chaos', to a totally chaotic state. Consider then the type of conversations that you have experienced in the past in this way. If your connection with somebody in a conversation is low, you are not listening fully or engaged, then the conversation will stagnate. If you, or the person you are talking to, puts up a defensive wall, unwilling to show any emotion or share their feelings, there will be no building of understanding or any opportunity to explore new ideas. Once you are able to start sharing your feelings and challenge each other's understanding then the connection will grow and new patterns of conversation will emerge.

In his writing on innovation, Jose Fonseca (2002: 52) highlights the role of misunderstanding in prompting new thinking. The search for resolution of the misunderstanding, rather than causing a breakdown in communication, can strengthen the connection. People enter into a phase in the conversation where they are testing their understanding of what the other person is saying. Out of that exchange new ideas emerge that take the conversation off in a novel direction. The same effect can be achieved where the conversation becomes challenging. Engaging in a challenging conversation can require you to reassess your thinking. It requires you to defend your ideas, consider other points of view and potentially accept new directions. Misunderstanding and resolving conflicts of ideas is an integral part of any challenging conversation.

Strengthening connections, being able to express yourself freely and challenge each other's thinking moves the conversation towards the 'edge of chaos' where you are able to explore new ideas and bring about change. This is well illustrated by Ruth's story and her description of the turning point in her client conversations, as being 'let in' – the point where both Ruth and her clients are able to engage and the dialogue opens up. Her likening of this to learning to dance illustrates the point well. It is the point where the consciously repeated patterns of steps becomes wired into the unconscious and the dancers start expressing themselves; the point where feeling is given free reign and repeated stable patterns give way to creativity and innovation.

Jumping into the unknown

The history of division and conflict in Northern Ireland and the changes brought about by the peace process, leading to the so called Good Friday Agreement of 1998 provides an illustration of how difficult change can be when deep-rooted realities are challenged. The history of conflict in Ireland, primarily against English, and then British, rule goes back some 800 years (Kee, 2003: 15). Henry VIII and his daughter Elizabeth I were both exercised by opposition to the Crown. Oliver Cromwell's suppression of Irish Catholicism in 1649 and the defeat of the Catholic army by the forces of William of Orange in 1690 are but staging posts in a long and bloody history. The Anglo–Irish Treaty of December 1921 which split the country into two, an independent state of Ireland, or Eire, and the British ruled counties of Northern Ireland, did not bring an end to the conflict. The 25-year period known euphemistically as 'The Troubles' of paramilitary action in Northern Ireland and on the British mainland was the precursor to the eventual peace agreement.

With such a long history, the reality of those involved is inevitably deeply held. Successive generations have grown up with that history. Their reality is shaped by the stories of the conflict, from whichever background they come, coloured by the personal trauma of loss and the values and beliefs of long held religious persuasions. Regardless of the rights and wrongs of the arguments on either side, a rational, conscious approach would say that continued conflict would be counterproductive and only lead to further trauma. After such a long period of aggression the prospect of one side or the other winning outright was remote. An agreement to live peacefully together would be the only way forward, but a move that would mean a fundamental change in everyone's thinking and behaviour.

It is difficult to pin down exactly when or how such a change occurred, exactly when the conversations started. There was a series of contacts between Gerry Adams of the republican political party Sinn Fein, and John Hume of the unionist Social Democratic and Labour Party, in 1988, some ten years before the signing of the agreement. In December 1993 the British prime minister, John Major and the Irish Taoiseach, Albert Reynolds, signed the Downing Street Declaration. In the following year on 31 August, the Irish Republican Army, or IRA, declared a ceasefire. These events, though, were steps on the way to a change designed to cement a process of conversations (Kee, 2003: 282–291). It is those very conversations, the willingness to challenge deeply held beliefs, to expose one's unconscious reality to question, that builds understanding and trust and ultimately the strength of connection. The process of negotiating the changes necessary to reach the peace agreement in 1998 was difficult and went down to the wire. Gerry Adams was reported to have said, after the agreement, that there comes a point when 'you just have to jump together'. Where you have to just trust that through the understanding that you have established together you will be able to find a new way of living together by taking the chance and making the change. It is at the point where you choose to change and trust that the new way of working will emerge from the interaction that follows.

What has followed the Good Friday Agreement hasn't, by any means, been plain sailing but fortunately, so far, the continued conversations have allowed new solutions to emerge at each point of challenge.

Organisationally, any change involves a jump into the unknown. However carefully planned and researched a proposed change may be, the eventual outcome will be unknown at the point of making the change. There is a point in the process where you have to 'jump together' into the unknown: the point where you expose your reality and confront the fear of change and trust in the strength of your connections for a new way to emerge. Jim's story in Chapter 1 of how he changed and flourished illustrates his jump into the unknown. Confronted by his long-held beliefs that he was not good enough due to his lack of height, he made the choice, there and then, to make a change. He made the choice to bring his unconscious belief into the conscious present and to act to change it. How that would work out was unknown. He did not know how he would get to the point of having the confidence to delegate work and the thought of carrying out one-to-one conversations with his staff was daunting. What he did was to choose to take a leap into the unknown. Through the conversations with his staff that followed, connections and understanding were formed from which a new way of working emerged.

In considering how we make the choice to change we have highlighted the importance of conversations and particularly those that are open and challenging. The sort of conversations that bring our values and beliefs, arising from our unconscious reality, into conscious focus and allow us to challenge and reform them. We have looked at how strengthening our connections with the individuals in our networks, through the understanding gained in those conversations, moves the system towards the 'edge of chaos', promoting the emergence of new ways of working.

In Jim's and Ruth's stories we have used narrative to provide an insight into what happens in a change situation, from a complexity perspective, paying attention to what was actually happening rather than to what management theory would say ought to be happening. In the next chapter we look a little closer at the power of storytelling in the shaping and reshaping of one's reality.

References

Fonseca, J. 2002. *Complexity and Innovation in Organizations.* Routledge: London.
Kauffman, S. 1995. *At Home in the Universe.* Penguin: London.
Kee, R. 2003. *Ireland: A History.* Abacus: London.

6   Storytelling
The power and influence of narrative learning

Paying attention to what is actually happening in organisations has brought us to see them as patterns of complex interaction between individuals. Mead's work has shown us the ways that we communicate as human beings through language and all the nuances of body language. Inherent in that communication is what Mead describes as gesture and response whereby we experience the feelings of others and respond accordingly. The study of neuroscience has highlighted our propensity to mirror the emotions of those we communicate with and create the group behaviours such as those that Bion identified. Finally, the theory of complex responsive processes brings these threads together to describe the emergent, unpredictable but recognisable patterns of behaviour in organisations. In this chapter, we look at the two distinct forms of learning, propositional and narrative, and consider how the way we learn from each other relates to the way we continually form and reform our personal realities; and how that influences the choices we make in the living present in creating our future.

Moving from narrative to propositional knowledge

The development of language has been key to the evolution of the human race. It gave humans not only the ability to communicate with their fellow beings but also to express their thoughts and reflect on their situation. The unique attribute of the human brain, in the pre-frontal lobes' ability to make conscious judgements of the future, gives us the opportunity to make choices in life.

Up until the end of the Middle Ages, a person's destiny was perceived as largely determined by fate. Their concept of the future was of one determined by the gods, and much time and effort was spent in pleasing them to ensure that things would turn out well. So little was presumed to be under human control, and planning for the future was not part of everyday life. In those times, learning and the fund of knowledge built up over the centuries was based on narrative – the tradition of storytelling that is handed down from generation to generation. Stories were recounted by the spoken word and wrapped up in the morality of the time.

With the advent of the Renaissance, the study of science and mathematics gained pace and the development of probability theory and the assessment of risk brought about the establishment of the insurance industry in London. The growth of trade at this time also brought a need to be able to assess markets and manage activities to deliver goods to those markets. This spurred on the study of probability and the use of past experience to predict the future.

The projection of past experience gains expression in the form of propositional knowledge and learning. This is the form of knowledge that assumes direct cause and effect: If this has happened, then that will follow. If I do this, then that will be the outcome. Previously, the use of narrative knowledge had been based largely on a collective understanding espoused in stories and metaphors. Narrative knowledge was passed on by the spoken word, related to local experience and was based on a contextual understanding of morality and purpose. That is, the stories evoke in the listener an understanding that has meaning in their own lives. So, in neurological terms, you are able, in hearing a story, to put it into the context of your own reality. Stories speak to the individual, engaging both the conscious and unconscious brain.

The increasing reliance on propositional knowledge since the Renaissance, reflects the focus of the time on Protestant and capitalist ethics, moral accountability, individual responsibility and the value of labour. The period of history covering the late fifteenth to the early seventeenth century across Europe and the sixteenth century in England was one of great change. The Renaissance brought the rebirth of interest in learning; it drew on the works and thinking of the classical period and encompassed the arts, philosophy, politics and science. The Protestant Reformation of the mid-sixteenth century challenged the assumption that salvation came solely from the grace of God and emphasised individual responsibility and divine forgiveness. The Protestant ethics of thrift and abstinence focused attention on the future as something that could be planned and worked for. The expansion of trade and the opportunity to gain wealth from industry promised rewards for this change in thinking. The propositional form of knowledge came to prominence because it described a thought process that is based on the assumption of action and reaction. Isaac Newton's formulation of the laws of motion, in the mid-seventeenth century, linked force with reaction. So, if the starting condition and the force applied are both known and charted, then the outcome can be predicted.

These ideas form the core of modern thought. The idea that outcomes can be forecast, regardless of the unpredictability of the environment, is part of modern culture. It is a part of everyday thinking that we can forecast the weather; but despite the ever-increasing sophistication of computer models we continue to be surprised. This form of thought process was accompanied by the developments of the scientific world in the pursuit of universal laws, an endeavour that encouraged the notion that the unpredictable elements of the environment should be discounted to arrive at a definitive law. Newton, in defining his laws of motion, disregarded friction as being too unpredictable.

The education system of the Western world is based on such Newtonian principles. The classical view of research is to propose a hypothesis, then carry out measurements and tests of that hypothesis to demonstrate its soundness for application. Provided nothing is found to disprove the theory then it is deemed not to be falsifiable and stands until such time as something is found. The desired outcome is a hypothesis, theory or law that can then be used to predict future behaviour or be used to govern an outcome. Management theory, as we saw in Chapter 2, has followed this route in the pursuit of the secret of organisational success, the most efficient structure and the ultimate management system.

Rule-based thinking

The principle of the 'if–then' sequence is further reinforced by the prominence of computer-based systems. The basic architecture of the computer is reliant on the binary nature of digital systems that know only two states, on or off. The electronic setting of any component is either positive or negative, on or off, activated or not activated. The use of binary functions in computer processors is a sophisticated science that relies on patterns of logic following a series of 'if–then' questions. Electronic systems based on rules that say, if the current setting of the switch is on then do this, or, if it is off then do that, are the basis of all procedures, rules and modern-day expert systems.

The ultimate extension of the propositional knowledge argument is the belief of many in artificial intelligence and its ability to replicate the functions of the human brain. The theory of artificial intelligence relies on the assumption that the human brain acts in a completely rational way and the reaction of an individual to any given situation is based on a fixed memory of past experience. Success, in these terms would simply be a matter of producing a machine which is fast enough to handle a sufficiently large memory database that will make the same level of informed choice as is available to the human brain.

Propositional knowledge is context-specific; it is a rule-based process founded on past experience of how to deal with defined situations by following learned rules. Contrary to this, narrative knowledge is the understanding that is communicated by stories where learning is based on drawing analogies that the listener can place in the context of their own past experience. Narrative knowledge may not be able to be disproved, in a scientific sense, but it carries individual meaning and flexibility in its context. So, the meaning to be gained from a narrative is not context-specific but contained in the understanding or the moral of the tale as it applies to our own situation.

The move to propositional knowledge was contemporary with the spread of the written word made possible by the invention of the printing press. The ability to then publish texts widely allowed the dissemination of the presumed universal laws and changed the focus of learning from the spoken word to the written word. This brought about the application of national laws rather than local consensus and customs, and it is the same process that now facilitates the procedural basis of management.

Although the use of procedures, rules and laws in organisations and society is accepted and propositional knowledge is ingrained by 300 years of positivist education, the informal communication channels still flourish and unwritten learning underlies much of human behaviour. The storytelling, the learning by analogy and through the knowledge of others' mistakes that is captured by those stories, carries a wisdom that is far richer than pure logic. Whilst propositional knowledge works from the application of rules derived from past observation to determine future action, narrative knowledge takes interpretations, analogy and metaphor to draw parallels from past experience with current situations and point to possible alternative courses of action. Narrative knowledge, in a modern context, is the way that we fill the gaps between the rules. However extensive the systems of rules and procedures are, they cannot cope with every eventuality.

Narrative, paradox and perception

The everyday world is a complex interrelationship between individuals, all of whom follow a social and personal agenda of self-interest. Behaviour is governed by perceptions derived from experience and the resolution of paradox and conflicting emotions from birth. We all face the eternal paradox of a drive to survive and the uniquely human condition of hope for the future whilst facing the inevitability of death. In life, we are constantly faced with contradictions like that. Situations where things happen to exist that seem to be contradictory. The feeling that an emotion is bittersweet or the idea that you may have to be cruel to be kind. In a social context, together we form society but at the same time we are being formed by it.

Shakespeare uses the device of being cruel to be kind to justify why Hamlet should kill his mother, reasoning that it would be better for her to be dead rather than be in love with his father's murderer. Such a paradox does not have a rational if–then solution, but it is in the telling of the story that an understanding and holding of the contradiction is possible. The interpretation of such anomalies requires an underlying knowledge of the wider context that is derived from storytelling.

The definition of propositional and narrative forms of knowledge relates to ways in which understanding is formulated, principally in terms of its transmission between individuals and the ways in which these individuals are able to apply or interpret that knowledge in a new context. In Chapter 3 we drew on neuroscience to see how we build our individual realities from birth. That reality, our understanding of the world, is retained by the brain in the patterns of neurons and their connections in the unconscious brain, and determines the way in which we react to new situations. So, our perception of the world is a creation of the reality held in the unconscious brain. It is a perception only partly based on the image landing on the retina, as the interpretation of that image is shaped by the expectation of your unconscious brain that the image will fit with the expected reality. That expected reality is reformed as the present image is compared and reinterpreted. The hardwired neural patterns in the unconscious brain are formed and reformed by experience and are the means by which we make sense of what we experience, every day, in the living present. Similarly, storytelling provides a way that we can compare the experience that is being conjured up by the story with our current understanding of the world, and reshape our reality accordingly.

When we hear the spoken word, as with sight, we are simply receiving sound waves in our ears which are then transmitted to our brain as electrical impulses. As infants, we learned that certain patterns of those impulses carried meaning. Then, as we learned to repeat those sounds, we were able to communicate our feelings and needs. We learned a language that enabled us to connect and interact with others in a meaningful way. The particular language that we learn, the meaning that we attach to specific sound patterns, clearly depends on which language is spoken by those around us and especially those who are caring for us at that young age. The patterns of neural firing which represent particular meanings to us are wired into our unconscious brain as a part of our personal reality. Speech and the understanding of what is said to us becomes automatic so we don't have to think about how we say things or what it means.

When we are interacting with someone and are engaged in conversation, the patterns of neural firing in our brain are constantly being compared with those experienced previously and meaning is being attached. The meaning that we attach to particular patterns, those produced by the words spoken, is, in part, a learned social construction. The common use of words in particular circumstances assigns meanings that we all internalise and share. At the same time through that the meaning is set in your personal context. For example, the word 'dog' as used in the English language and culture is commonly understood to represent a particular type of domesticated family pet or working animal. We all know what we mean by the word. However, our personal experience, the hardwired reality built up in our unconscious brain, will bring forward particular emotions and unconscious reactions. The word may evoke feelings of companionship and affection related to a loved family pet. For another, the word may cause feelings of insecurity and fear from an experience of feeling threatened by a dog at an early age.

In general, the words spoken in a conversation will carry a unique and particular meaning for each of us. Together with the emotions evoked and the unconscious mirroring response, the way we respond will be unpredictable, both in ourselves and the expectation of others, and continually emerging. We are all engaged in a continuous and constantly emerging process of sense making as we interact and communicate with each other. This is the ongoing gesture and response described by Mead, the basis of Stacey's 'complex responsive processes of human relating', and the way in which we negotiate our lives in organisations.

Communicating in organisations

Communication, we are told, on an almost daily basis, is vitally important to the success of organisations. Every management training course will stress the need for effective communication. Every good change management programme should include a communications plan, one that will set out what the key messages are to be, what channels of communication are to be employed and by whom, and how we ensure that the message has been received and understood. But despite all this, the most common complaint in change programmes and across organisations is that the communication was poor. It is a key part of the narrative in Chapter 1. Almost from the beginning there was doubt about the adequacy of the communication and a focus on what they thought that they were not being told.

So, what is actually happening in organisations when we are communicating?

There are numerous business courses that will tell you that effective communication is essential for success. Predominantly these courses will focus on what might be termed as the mechanics of communicating. Maintaining clarity and avoiding ambiguity, clear voice projection and active listening, reflecting back what you have heard in order to avoid any misunderstanding, are all set out as key skills. Awareness of what your body language is saying and the tone of your spoken delivery is necessary to ensure your meaning is understood, and displaying empathy and respect are important. All of these things are important; however, they tend to relate to the transmission and receipt of a message rather than the sense-making process of a conversation. The fact that these skills are stressed is symptomatic of how we view formal communication in organisations. Vision and mission statements, reports, policies, guidance notes, procedures, rules and regulations, whether in hard or soft copy, these written communications are the foundation of organisational management. They are propositional in nature, e.g. if your company policy is breached then disciplinary action will follow; or purely directional, e.g. you must follow the safety regulations at all times. Where views are expressed, perhaps in a mission statement, they tend to be expressed as though they are views held by the organisation rather than the individuals who make up the company. The context is general, relating to the organisation as a whole, or a part of it, such that the instruction or the message can be applicable to all. The transmission of the information is also, generally, one-way and from one person to many. Even in the case of a spoken presentation this sort of process seems to apply, often with the visual content reduced to a series of bullet points to be delivered. In all cases the received wisdom is that the message should be clear, unambiguous and understood by all, so that 'we are all on the same page' and 'all singing from the same hymn sheet'.

If we look, though, at what is actually happening we get a different perspective. All communications originate from a particular individual. They may have been drafted by one person and edited by many but the final version that is communicated will carry the voice of the person that wrote it. It will come from the personal reality of that individual. Whilst it may be read, or spoken as in the case of a presentation or speech, it will be received by individuals. Whether the message is spoken or written, delivered in person or simply distributed it will carry with it body language or tone of expression that will speak to the unconscious reality of the recipient. Each will put that message into the context of their own experience and expectations of the future.

Let's think about the instance where the chief executive of an organisation addresses her staff, perhaps at an annual conference, to set out her vision of the future for the organisation. After careful consideration and refinement, she will address her speech to the gathered audience. She will have taken care to ensure that her words are clear and unambiguous and that her appearance and delivery are appropriate. She will be keen to convey her enthusiasm for the successful future of the organisation to all members of her audience. It will appear to her that she is addressing everyone in her audience with the same message. If she is a skilled orator she will be at pains to, or at least to appear to, make eye contact with every individual, trying to ensure that she has everyone on board and behind a clear message. But however skilled she may be at making eye contact with everybody, she is not addressing a uniform group of people. She is actually having a large number of individual conversations.

The chief executive's words, finely crafted, will have been filtered by her reality, and equally, will be received in the same way. Every individual listening will put those words into their own context and make their own unique sense of what she is saying. As the unconscious part of the brain reacts much faster than the conscious part there will be an instant reaction. That reaction, of each individual in the audience, will be picked up by those around them. Words may be spoken by people adjacent to each other and their emotional responses will be mirrored. In the same way that an actor picks up the mood of the audience without a word being spoken from the auditorium, the chief executive will get an emotional response to her address. There is a process of gesture and response emerging from the internal, and largely unconscious, unspoken conversation between the speaker and the audience.

Once the address is completed the sense making process will continue. The chief executive will return to her office and her circle of advisors. The individuals from her audience will go back to their own places within the organisation and conversations around the meaning of the address will continue. Every individual has a limited circle of colleagues with whom they interact on a regular basis. Usually these are people that they know well, maybe having worked with them for some time. The conversations, in this context, will tend to be of a narrative nature, perhaps:

'Well what did you think of her plans to expand the business?'

'I remember when this was proposed last time and it was a nightmare. We all ended up doing twice as much work with no extra pay!'

As the individuals will all be members of many groups within the organisation, the conversation will connect everybody. In this way, through the ongoing process of gesture and response in conversations across the organisation, and beyond as family and friends become part of a wider conversation, a pattern of sense-making will emerge. Such an emerging pattern, as we have seen with complex networks of conversations, will be unpredictable. The intended clear and unambiguous message will become a general understanding that, for the chief executive, is entirely unpredictable and unknowable at the outset.

Using narrative forms of communication

So, whilst the formal communication process in organisations is essentially propositional, the form of learning that makes sense of the communication is narrative. In the same way, it is the narrative conversations that make sense of all the policies, rules and regulations that an organisation sets in place to manage and control the behaviour of its individuals. When it comes to making laws on a national level, politicians and their advisors will pay great attention to drafting the words to go on the statute, again striving to make them clear and unambiguous. However, when it comes to interpreting the meaning of laws we rely on the courts and the precedents of previous cases that been heard. The form of learning employed then is narrative. The parties to the case each tell their story to the court and the jury or the judge will make sense of that in their own context. When it comes to understanding the rules of an organisation it is generally through a narrative process that we make sense of the regulations and decide how to act.

The most common and effective use of narrative learning in organisations is in the training room. Formal training is predominantly propositional. The purpose of a training course is to teach you how to recognise a situation where a particular action is necessary and provide you with the tools, techniques and skills needed to deal with it: it's a simple 'if–then' process. The structure and presentation used in training, usually set out in bullet lists, is propositional. If you need to improve your communication skills then you need to do this, be aware of that and act in this way. The effective learning, though, is in the stories used by the trainer to illustrate the point.

In the health and safety training that I have delivered in my career in the construction industry I have often used the following story to illustrate points around personal protection and risk.

Having graduated from college in 1975 with a degree in civil engineering I embarked on a career working as a site engineer. I was employed on a heavy engineering site in Scunthorpe where the project was to construct an extension to the vast billet rolling mill at the steelworks. With the mill's existing length of around a mile and a half, the extension was a mere quarter mile long. We were working at the end of the working mill, constructing a large steel structure the size of an aircraft hangar, with heavy reinforced concrete foundations to carry the rolling machinery. The new structure was being built on an area of the steelworks that had previously been excavated as a quarry, so the steel piles that were needed to support the foundations had to be some 30–40 metres in length. As these piles were being produced on site and therefore didn't have to be transported by road, they could be driven complete, using specially extended rigs. This required a rigger to climb to the top of the pile guide and, once the pile was in place, to secure and tighten the bolts on the frame holding the top of the pile. The convention, known to the rest of the piling crew, was that the rigger would bang on the pile with his spanner before dropping it, thereby saving him having to carry the spanner whilst descending the rig's ladder. At this time, the ink was still fresh on the Health and Safety Act of 1974, so paying attention to the risks involved in this act was not commonplace.

Having completed my activities for the afternoon I was returning to the site office amidst the noise, and unaware that the particular sound of banging on the rig was a warning to stand clear of the falling spanner. As I was approaching the rig I was narrowly missed by the heavy eighteen-inch spanner as it landed in front of my feet. As it happened I was wearing a safety helmet but I'm sure that, had I been struck, I would have sustained a serious injury.

The propositional point here is straightforward. If you are in an area where falling spanners, or any other objects, are a danger then you need to have adequate risk assessments, procedures and protective clothing. Presenting the point in a narrative, however, presents a context which can be taken up by the listener and engages with their unconscious reality.

The experience of that event has become a part of my reality. My subsequent involvement with health and safety over the years, working in risk assessment and procedures and repeated telling of the story in the training room, has prompted me to revisit my perceptions of the event and reformed my reality as a result. In telling the story, I can see the site, the piling rig, and remember noise, the smell of diesel and the feeling of shock as the spanner landed at my feet. But my perceptions of the incident have changed over the years as my understanding of the risks has developed; yet the context remains. The reality that I have built around the experience is unique to myself but by putting it into a story in the training session, others are enabled to create their reality by putting it into their own context. I'm sure that in reading this story you will have created, in your mind, a picture of what I have described. Even if you have never been on a construction site you will have used the knowledge that you have of them from pictures, videos or other accounts you have come across to give your context to the story. It is often said that the best pictures are those on the radio. Those pictures that are conjured up from your imagination, in response to a story. A context that you have given to the narrative built out of your past experiences. That story and the accompanying context then becomes a part of your reality. Stored away in the neural patterns of your unconscious brain, that learning will continue to influence your thinking, often unknown to your conscious self, for the future. I was struck, over the years, by listening to the stories told informally by the construction workers and how they learned from each other. The recounting of events from the past, particularly those of accidents and near misses, provided an ongoing and very powerful learning forum. Younger workers picked up as much, if not more, about the do's and don'ts of site safety here as they did from the formal training courses. Lessons that were far more durable due to the narrative format. This, largely unacknowledged, learning process was a natural part of the everyday life on site and is replicated generally across all organisations.

In the spanner story, there was a lack of understanding on my behalf of the meaning of the signal from the top of the rig. In this case, the communication was not by way of a verbal warning. There was a gesture from the rigger at the top of the rig in the form of a banging on the pile with the sound carried down the steel pile to ground level. The response expected by the rigger was that the area that he was dropping the spanner into would be cleared. Nowadays, a thorough risk assessment would have identified that there was a serious risk attached to that procedure. I'm sure that the dropping of the spanner would not now be permitted; however, the story illustrates how misunderstanding can result when the unconscious memory is not wired to respond to the given gesture. As you will probably be aware from the last time you inadvertently touched something hot, the unconscious reaction is the immediate reaction. The conscious realisation that it was hot comes a little later.

What is actually happening when we are communicating in organisations is a mix of propositional and narrative learning. The propositional to formulate and disseminate the formal processes and procedures of the organisation; the narrative to make sense of those communications. We are using storytelling and the narrative form of the informal conversations to fill in the gaps in the formal rules. We are using storytelling to enable us to put the learning into a personal context and absorb it into our unconscious reality.

Communicating in change

As with everyday communication in an organisation, the process of managing change also places great emphasis on the need for clear communication, the need for a communication strategy that clearly articulates what is changing and what the benefits will be for the organisation and the individuals. Such a strategy should address the practical aspects of the message that will be communicated, for example what channels, such as presentations, meeting notes and electronic media, should be used, which audiences need to be addressed and what should be the process for governance and review.

Most important is the need to set out how things will be in the future, identify the gains to be made by all and report on the progress being made. Whilst the use of storytelling and arresting imagery in assisting the communication of the message is encouraged, the message is, however, focused on creating a vision of the future and persuading individuals to move towards it. The message will be processed by the conscious brain, as it is forward looking and rational. As that is happening, though, the unconscious brain will have already made its response. The gut feelings of anxiety, scepticism and fight-or-flight reactions will set in before the conscious awareness of future benefits has had time to settle.

We saw in Jim's story of change in Chapter 1 that it was not the formal communications about the change programme that dominated his thinking and the conversations of his staff. Those conversations were not about how much better the future will be, as set out in the formal presentations, but were based on fears about the present that were driven by their past experience. The works supervisor worried about what he saw as a challenge to his expertise, asking 'What do they know about trucks?' There were concerns over what they feared would lead to extra work. The positive part of the ongoing conversation, that Jim refers to a number of times, is the reminder of their past success in taking on board change in the previous takeover. Referring to the past reality of success allowed Jim to speak directly to the past experience of change in his staff. A memory stored in the unconscious and associated with feelings of success prompts an immediate response which will be mirrored by the others.

In any change programme there is a need to identify and communicate what the future state of the organisation is intended to be, to inform individuals about how the change will affect their future roles and activities. All that needs to be set out clearly and unambiguously. But to carry those individuals with us into that future state we need to address their current reality and allow them to reform that reality. As the conscious brain catches up with the unconscious response to the message there is a tendency to impose a rational explanation. Jim's work supervisor rationalised his refusal to engage with the process by insisting that 'It will never work.' In neurological terms, this is an example of one's implicit attitude coming into conflict with the explicit. With the implicit attitude being deeply rooted in the unconscious memory it will tend to dominate and the logic of all the benefit that may be offered will not be accepted. The result is to prompt a seemingly irrational resistance to the planned change. The communication process then needs to speak first to the implicit attitude of each individual. To focus on evoking positive memories of past success in change situations and reforming individual realities such that they are enabled to change.

So, in Jim's story, at the start of the change programme he talks to his staff and tries to reassure them that they will be able to work with the change, citing their success in dealing with change in the previous takeover of their old firm. In this way, he was appealing to the feelings of past success in managing change, something that had become a part of their individual realities.

In our final chapter, we turn to what our alternative view of change means for the practice of change management. We will consider how we can work with individuals to enable them to make a positive choice, in the present, to change. How we can strengthen the connectivity between those individuals and move the network towards the 'edge of chaos' where innovative change is possible.

7 Putting choice at the centre of change management
Easing the path to change

What do we really mean when we talk about change management? Indeed, is it actually possible to manage change? It is, of course, perfectly possible to implement a change. On a personal level, we can move our career in a different direction by taking a new job, we can buy a new car or move to an exotic location to live. These things all take a degree of planning to achieve successfully and in that respect, they have to be managed. Socially, we can enact new laws and change regulations, and individually we can change how we live. In organisations, we can implement change, we can introduce a new IT system, we can change working practices and procedures or we can restructure the organisation. All these changes also need to be planned, communicated and managed in a practical sense if they are to be successful.

However, as Ruth observes in Chapter 4:

> No matter what the rationale for the change and how positive it may potentially be, you can't anticipate how people, in their day-to-day jobs, will respond to opportunities.

Her story tells of the resistance to the use of computers that she encountered in trying to introduce them into P&F Ltd in the early 1990s. The issues lay not in the practical change itself but in the assent, or otherwise, of the people who were being asked to make a change in the way they saw the world, a change that affected their reality.

This sort of response is echoed in Jim's story of how he and his staff experienced change. The issues raised there were not rational objections to what they were being asked to do. It was not a case of, 'If we change the way we do this particular activity it will have this negative effect.' The challenges raised were in defence of their personal reality by questioning the knowledge and credibility of the consultants implementing the change. In both of these examples, those being asked to change were not making rational decisions not to comply but unconscious choices to maintain their current reality.

Choosing to change

When we talk about change management then, in organisations, we are not talking about change in terms of project management, the practical aspects of changing practice, we are dealing with matters of choice. Change, in any context, will only be effective if those involved make the choice to make that change. A conscious choice that allows the reforming of their unconscious reality.

It is, of course, possible to make almost anybody change their ways if sufficient pressure is brought to bear. In the extreme, a threat to them or their loved ones' lives or some form of blackmail may well bend people to one's will. So when we talk about change management we have to consider it as a practice that brings about change in a situation where people have choice. A process of changing reality by consent.

A few years ago I was fortunate enough to spend a couple of years working in Perth, Western Australia. In common with the rest of the country, surfing was a very popular sport there. At the same time, the waters of the Indian Ocean in that part of the world are known hunting grounds for dangerous sharks. Over the period that we lived in Perth there were several attacks, some of them fatal. There are, of course, risks in pretty much everything that we do as part of our daily lives. On average over the past ten years seven people have died every day on the roads of Great Britain. As a proportion of all the people making a journey each day that number is very small but nevertheless every time we take to the roads we accept that risk. In modern life, many of those journeys are unavoidable but that cannot be said of surfing in water frequented by sharks. So what makes people choose to take a significant risk that they don't have to face?

In Chapter 3 we looked at the work of Herbert Mead and the contemporary studies of neuroscience to understand what drives us to act as we do in the present. We saw that how we act in the present emerges from the coincidence of our current perceptions of our past experience and our expectations of the future. For the surfer, standing on Mullaloo Beach, Perth, thinking of entering the water, her choice will take her unconscious back to all the times she has experienced the adrenalin rush of past rides. It will evoke those feelings of hearing the news of shark attacks in the past. She will anticipate the feelings of the exhilaration to come from getting on to her surfboard and the fear of what could happen in the worst case. The decision to enter the water or to turn back is a split second one. Neurological research (Eagleman, 2011: 167) has shown that the unconscious brain has acted to direct your response well before the conscious brain has engaged with the issue. The surfer's action, in the moment, is emergent from her current reality not a considered decision.

To say, then, that change is a matter of choice and that it is essentially an unconscious and largely irrational act would seem to imply that change management is at best ill-conceived or at worst a waste of time. We see, though, from the narratives of change here, that benefits did arise from the programme implemented in Jim's company, not least for Jim himself, and that there was a definite need for the employees of P&F Limited to change in the face of external pressures. How should we reconcile these positions?

Revisiting resistance to change

We considered first how the management view of the change process has developed over the course of the twentieth century and is now the dominant thinking on how change management should be done. The view of organisations 'as-if' they act like machines, bounded systems working in linear, cause and effect relationships is symptomatic of that way of thinking. From that, we have a process-led approach based in Lewin's three stages of unfreeze, change and refreeze. Change management is seen very much as a project to be managed, with great stress being placed on the need for planning and communication.

Jim's story of change, in Chapter 1, refers to the change programme in his organisation having a planned and structured approach. The changes to be made, the measures and KPIs to be introduced had all been determined by an initial phase of assessment and trial. A communications pack had been created to inform and reassure people about the change and a training programme had been delivered. Although the impact, in Jim's case, of the communication and the training seems to have not been particularly memorable, they had attempted to address the first stage of unfreezing the organisation. The key parts of the story relate to the implementation, or change, phase. A consultant was assigned to the depot with a brief to implement a series of changes in the way the business was run, setting up regular meetings, conference calls between all the depots on the programme and the one-to-one meetings. A set of key performance indicators were established to measure the efficiency of the business and provide a reporting mechanism on the benefits being gained from the programme. Beyond introducing the new processes, the role of the consultant was 'to coach the staff ... and work with individual staff members through the change'.

The change cycle was employed as a device to show how the change was being 'refrozen' as the new way of working. The extent to which the change was being accepted as the norm.

Jim's experience of the change programme in relation to his Southeast Depot was that it was largely successful. The efficiency measures improved things, and as he says '[by the end of the programme] we were absolutely flying ... everybody had bought into it and it was a happy place'. This was despite the fact that two members of staff had been lost who could not make the choice to accept the change. For Jim, the programme had proved to be a game changer: '[it has] made me a better person, made me a better manager'. However, as he found when he visited the West London Depot, there 'it was still quite negative. Although they had been through the same programme, with the same people, so why was it so different there?'

There is a lot written about the failure of change management programmes. Research surveys have come up with a range of percentages but commonly suggest that a substantial majority of programmes fail, when measured against the original objectives. Similarly, the reasons given for the failures are many and various, but the most often cited can be grouped into the following two areas:

- Lack of a clear vision and failure to communicate that vision and the benefits of change.
- Failure to adequately plan the delivery and implementation of the change and a lack of leadership, particularly by top management.

Failure to successfully manage change is generally seen as, not a failure of process or underlying assumptions but one of execution. It was not the way the change was approached but a lack of effective project management or decisive leadership.

Much of the commentary on problems faced in change management is devoted to the issue of resistance, of those who are seen as somehow putting unnecessary obstacles in the path of a smooth transition from the old to the new way of working. Such people are often referred to in pejorative terms, 'blockers' being a common expression. The finance director of P&F, in Ruth's story, who rejected all computers as 'Japanese junk', would probably fit that description. Some of his colleagues who less emphatically rejected the idea of introducing computers, saying 'it would be perfect, but not for them, not for their department or not for their situation', could be considered in the same way. There are, no doubt, some people, who for personal or political reasons want to prevent change from happening. Maybe from some form of grudge against the company and feelings of resentment from their position. My experience is though, and it would seem to be the case with the finance director, that those who resist change do not have any explicit, rational plan to block change. They are simply responding to an unconscious feeling of threat to their reality. In the case of the finance director, a threat to his very sense of being.

The approach to dealing with resistance from the managed change perspective is, again, to see the issue as one of execution rather than a fault in process. The problem is supposed to be with those blocking change rather than those proposing it or the way that they are interacting with the former. This view, arising from the scientific management philosophy, leads you to the conclusion that something has to be done to deal with the person who is resisting the change. The person must somehow be 'got around', removed or persuaded of the error in their thinking. Such an approach will, maybe, work in the short term but is unlikely to satisfy the needs of the individual for long. As Ruth observes, 'it isn't possible to pre-determine what the future should be when the reality of those involved in any change is constantly changing and often in ways completely hidden from our understanding'.

The dominant view of leadership, in respect of managing change, tends to the heroic, where change is something that is done to those who are required to change. The forms of leadership advocated for managing change cover the full range from autocratic to consensual. As noted in the common reasons for failure, strong top-down leadership, whether that is transactional, charismatic or transformational, is seen as essential to success.

Jim's story acknowledges the involvement of top management in the programme and their participation in the conference calls, though he does question the strength of the commitment of some in the process. It is, however, at the level of middle management, his line manager the operations manager, where he identifies a difference between his own depot and the West London one that he worked with later. Jim notes the positive attitude of his manager, saying:

> He was fully involved both with the programme and its implementation at the depot level. He did the one-to-ones for his reports. He was involved in and did the observations and quality checks. He was always coming to the depot, talking to people.

That was not the case with the West London Depot, and it was not until Jim was dispatched there and was able to 'have a quite open and frank discussion about what they were doing and what they were going to do' that things began to improve. '[Now], it's one of the company's better locations'.

Organisations as they are observed to be

We turned then in Chapter 3 to the view of what is actually happening in an organisation, the nature of change and how employees make the choice to change. Using an understanding derived from the study of the behaviour of non-linear networks, Mead's work on the patterns of gesture and response and contemporary neuroscience, we formed an alternative view to the scientific model of organisational behaviour, a view that accepts that organisations are essentially just groups of individuals interacting and doing their best to deliver their shared goals. A view that accepts that individuals are unpredictable in how they will react, and that organisational life is therefore messy, in the sense that it does not follow neat, logical and systematic patterns and the outcome of all the ongoing interaction is emergent and individually unknowable. This approach does not seek to describe organisations 'as-if' they are some form of determinate system but treats them 'as-is', that is, as they are observed to be.

The study of complex adaptive systems provides us with an analogy for what happens in organisations. That is not to say that organisations behave 'as-if' they are complex adaptive systems. It is by observing how patterns of behaviour emerge from non-linear networks of interacting individuals that we can draw parallels with what we see in organisations.

We saw from Mead's work and the study of neuroscience how we all, as individuals acting in a social setting, are driven by our unconscious reality, the reality that is constructed from our exploration of the world around us and our experiences over the years. How we react to our ever-changing environment and the gestures continually being made by those around us, is determined by that reality and our expectation of the future. As a result of the speed with which our unconscious brain reacts, compared to the considered process of our conscious brain, the response we make, in the present, is not the rational, logical one that we would like to think. The sequence of gesture and response that is our ongoing conversation is unpredictable and its outcome unknowable from the outset. But at the same time, it can be rich and creative. Organisations are then groups of individuals interacting continually through conversations and producing changing patterns of unpredictable and potentially innovative behaviour.

Through the modelling of complex adaptive systems and observation of the behaviour of similar processes in reality, such as the motorway traffic example or the emergence and fading away of changing dress codes in organisations, we get an insight into how people react to change. Computer simulation demonstrates how self-organisation and recognisable patterns of behaviour emerge from the networks where each individual is acting independently. Whilst they have shared sets of rules there is no overall design that is setting the patterns. We see, also, how there are attractors of behaviour, often buried deep in our shared genetic memory, which draw us unconsciously to certain reactions. The survival response of conserving energy leads us to the option requiring the least effort. Learning a new way of working requires us to work with our conscious brain to master the process and through repetition commit it to our unconscious reality. By resisting the change, we don't have to expend that effort. The avoidance of anxiety leads us into basic assumption behaviours, such as fight-or-flight reactions and the resistance of change where we might fail. Deeply held beliefs, like thinking that we are not good enough, bring a fear of change which overrides any rational reasons to change.

We see this clearly demonstrated in Ruth's story of her project to introduce computers to P&F. Although, individually, employees could see the logic of using computers, there was a collective fear of embracing the change. Nobody wanted to have them in their department or as part of their way of working.

In Jim's story, there is the emergence of a collective resistance. The conversations between the staff members served to reinforce their individual and very personally driven feelings about what was happening. Jim himself had considerable reservations about the changes and along with the workshop supervisor's reaction to the initial trials, an atmosphere of 'apprehension about the future' emerged, and 'They … went straight on to the defensive'.

Reforming realities

I recently had to travel from my home in South Lincolnshire to Thurso, on the north coast of Scotland, for business. This involved a journey of some 600 miles, a flight to Inverness and a hire car to travel the final 120 miles. At home I normally drive a car with an automatic gearbox, so, as we saw in Chapter 3, the unconscious reality that I have formed of how to drive a car does not involve operating a clutch and changing gear. The car I hired at Inverness, however, had a manual gearbox. So, rather than just getting into the car and driving away I had to make a conscious effort to get the car into gear and to move away smoothly. Whilst I was making that conscious effort things progressed reasonably well. But as soon as I got onto a stretch of open road and relaxed, my unconscious mode took back control and before I knew it I had stalled the engine and come to a halt at a roundabout. It took some time driving that car to get back into the habit of changing gear. My reality had to be reformed, if only briefly, to allow me to drive without needing to think about every gear change. Even after a couple of days it was still taking a degree of concentration for things to run without a hitch. As I was thinking about the writing of this book at the time, it was quite a clear example to me of how dominant one's unconscious thought process is and the conscious effort that is required to overcome its instant control.

Organisationally, we see this most clearly in Jim's account of his reality change. It is in his account of the one-to-one sessions, and in particular his experience in revisiting his values and beliefs, that a new pattern emerged and his embrace of the change process happened. It was here that Jim was able to bring his long-held belief about his lack of height leading to his inability to achieving success, into the open. By bringing that part of his unconscious reality into focus in his conscious mind he was able to reform his reality and make progress. He says:

> As the conversation opened out into some of the issues I was experien- cing in my work life, such as finding it difficult to delegate work or manage my long working days, I began to see things more clearly. Yes, I think it was the Values and Beliefs that brought it home to me that although I am only five feet six inches tall it doesn't matter.

We are constantly forming and reforming our reality. Jim's realisation that his height was not an issue in his aspirations dramatically changed his reality. His example is particularly remarkable in the change that it brought about but it does demonstrate a more general process that is happening all the time as we move forward. Having made that change, Jim's attitude to the change and the way that he conveyed that to his staff also changed. He noticed changes in the rest of his staff as they went through the same sessions, saying, 'they are more confident in the way they are doing their jobs'. As the conversations changed an acceptance of the change began to emerge in the depot and 'they never looked back'.

By contrast, at the West London Depot, it is Jim's view that, whilst subject to the same programme, it was their failure to take on board issues raised in their Values and Beliefs sessions that was holding them back. The story there, however, also tells of how in the one-to-ones, that Jim continued, the customer service manager addressed 'some of the issues raised by the Values and Beliefs'. As Jim relates, he became a 'changed person', more outgoing and able to engage with change, as in the taking on of a yard person.

So, we can now see organisations as ongoing emerging patterns of conversations based on the achievement of some shared intended outcome. In other words, groups of individuals who come together to produce something or provide a service by interacting with each other to that end. That interaction can only be through a sequence of gestures and responses, carried out through ongoing conversations, both verbal and non-verbal and by actions and responses, or what Ralph Stacey describes as complex responsive processes of human relating, in the living present, where the future is perpetually being constructed (Stacey, 2001: 173).

Throughout our two narratives we have seen a repeated theme of the importance of meaningful conversations. In Jim's story there were the one-to-one sessions and the focus on confronting our deeply held beliefs, his conversations with his staff and the improved communication offered by the conference calls. All these served to strengthen the influence of the connections between the individuals and prompt the emergence of a successful change.

Ruth's story contrasts the lack of engagement in meaningful conversations, about the issues in P&F, that may have led to the breakthrough effect of being 'let in' to more challenging emotions leading to new thinking. In P&F there was a view that 'If the future is uncertain, then what's the point in talking about it?' Whilst the lack of conversations about future challenges was not the ultimate reason for the company's failure, the lack of engagement created an insularity, a lack of interaction between the staff, that prevented the emergence of ways of dealing with the changes in their environment. Ruth concludes:

> That was something that I really took away from my experience at P&F. The importance not of just talking to people, having conversations, but having those sorts of challenging, opening, mind opening exploratory conversations in which you don't feel threatened. Where you can talk about things without feeling threatened or anxious.

It is the strength of the interaction in the ongoing conversations that is so important in moving networks towards the condition of being at the 'edge of chaos' where creativity is given expression, as we discovered in Chapter 5. We have seen how the tendency towards patching in natural networks and organisations has the effect of moving the network towards that 'edge of chaos', the point where the system produces new patterns of behaviour. Within a given arrangement of networks it is the strength of the interaction that moves the system to that point. In the terminology of complex adaptive systems, the strength of the connection between individuals acting in the network is the degree to which the actions of one agent influences the actions of those connected to it.

Challenging perceptions

We have seen from our narratives how challenging conversations can be the catalyst for change. Jim recounts how the conversation in his Values and Beliefs one-to-one was 'both difficult and a revelation'. He also recalls that the subsequent one-to-one meetings with his staff, whilst difficult for him at first, prompted him to ask questions that he had 'never really asked' before. Ruth reflects on her time with P&F and how difficult it was to involve people in challenging conversations, and on her consultancy role and how she used that approach to open up the real issues facing her clients. What, though, do we mean by engaging people in challenging conversations?

In the fifth century BCE Socrates used a form of challenging dialogue in searching for the true meaning of concepts such as courage, friendship and piety. Socrates was so wedded to the use of dialogue to seek truth, by questioning others, that he never actually wrote any of his thinking down, and it was left to his pupil Plato and others that followed him, to record his philosophy for posterity.

Socrates' approach was to ask a seemingly straightforward question, such as 'What is justice?' and to then question the response. In this way he would tease out the contradictions in the other person's thinking in an attempt to arrive at an unquestionable answer. It was Socrates' ultimate downfall that many among those that he questioned were unsettled by being left with far more uncertainty at the end of the conversation than they had started with, and this led to him being condemned to death, on a charge of corrupting the young, and his execution in 399 BCE.

This form of enquiry, known as Socratic dialogue, or perhaps more commonly as being the Devil's advocate, has become firmly embedded in western culture. It is a technique used in legal education to analyse court decisions and debate a judge's decisions. There are many management tools in modern organisational consulting that use this approach by repeatedly asking the question: Why? Having asked a person why they are doing something in a particular way, the response is then challenged by asking again, 'Why is that so?' Generally, it does not take many repetitions to get to the underlying reasons for people's actions and this often exposes behaviours that hadn't been recognised before.

So, to engage in a challenging conversation, in an organisational context, is not just a matter of the particular subject matter to be discussed but is about addressing the unconscious drivers of anxiety that are personal to those involved, such as the perceptions of low self-worth or the threat of redundancy from new technology that we have seen in the narratives. In the change situation those are the feelings that drive people to put up the barriers and prevent the engagement that will take them towards the 'edge of chaos' and new patterns of working.

It is often the challenge of being prompted to think differently or to face a difficult feeling that frees up the conversation, both internally and with others, and allows expression of new ideas. The example of the seminar in Ruth's narrative illustrates how, when confronted with a new way of thinking about their businesses, the attendees were able to step away from their preconceptions about business plans and take a new approach. For the client who was running a family business, whom we met in Chapter 4, it was Ruth's telling of her own story that allowed him to express and confront, his own feelings. In all of these examples the people involved were enabled to make a choice to change, a choice to move forward unconstrained by their perceptions of the past. The purpose of the challenging conversation, in all its forms, is to enable that choice, to allow people to be able to engage in the emerging patterns coming from the conversations and choose to take a step into the unknown.

The story of the signing of the Good Friday Agreement, following such a long and bitter struggle in Ireland, shows how pivotal making that choice to change is, to be able to move forward and work with the new patterns that flow from it. The ability to make that choice came not from military or political power but from the willingness to have the challenging conversations. This story also illustrates, here, the power of narrative. We explored in Chapter 6 how powerful the narrative form of communication, or storytelling, can be in learning. Even if you are not familiar with the history of the 'Troubles' in Ireland and the events that led to the Good Friday Agreement, the telling of the story in itself puts the point across about choosing to make such a leap of faith, and how that was enabled, in a context that can easily be understood.

Using narrative for change

Throughout the literature on change the importance of good communication is stressed. Taking the view, set out in Chapter 3, that organisations are simply groups of individuals interacting in pursuit of a shared goal, we recognise that ongoing gesture and response, particularly conversation, is the way that we all negotiate our lives in those organisations. Propositional, directive learning has an important place in organisations. There is always the need to tell people what is expected of them. But it is the narrative form of learning from each other's stories that facilitates our understanding of those directions. It is how we learn from each other 'how things work' and the way that we establish a shared understanding. It is how we interpret the paradoxes of everyday life.

The power of narrative learning comes from being able to put the story in to the context of your own experience. The narratives in this volume only exist in their original context for those who were there at the time, but we can all imagine the scene. Even if we haven't worked in similar organisations we all have some notion of what it is like, maybe from films or from the stories of others who have. We are able to characterise the people described in the stories from others we have met in the past. We create a version of the story in our heads based on our own reality, and what we learn from it will reshape that reality. In this way, narrative communication speaks directly to the reality of the recipient. The meaning derived by each individual from the story will depend on their particular reality and will be unpredictable and unknowable at the outset. Thus, open and challenging narrative conversations that are used to explore and reshape the individual realities of those engaged in them are the forums that lead to new understanding and emergent patterns of change.

In writing this book I have sought to set out an alternative view of change management, one that starts by accepting the nature of organisations as they are rather than proposing a predictive model of how they should work. Organisations as groups of individuals that aren't the rational logical beings that, perhaps, we would like to think that we are. We have seen that we are all complex people each driven by a very personal unconscious reality built up though our experiences from birth.

The extent of writing on the difficulties of delivering change in organisations is testament to the fact that the response of people to change is unknowable at the outset and unpredictable in the way it turns out. The high degree of resistance to change experienced in change projects is well documented and there are numerous theories written about how to overcome it. Ruth observes, in her story, how she

> found that trying to create the kind of motivation for change just by pointing out the problems doesn't necessarily mean that you are going to get the change.

Having said that, it has to be acknowledged that the conventional management approach to change is valid in the respect that to implement any change there has to be an idea of where you are trying to get to, a plan of how to do that and a process followed to implement the practical aspects. However, the established view of managing change is based on an approximation to the truth. An 'as-if' view of organisations that puts to one side the 'friction' of human interaction and assumes human rationality. To take account of these realities we need to accept that we cannot manage change in the conventional sense of defining and implementing a specified future state of being. The idea that we can set out a vision of a new way of working, communicate that in an unambiguous way and expect that to be taken up exactly as intended does not work out in practice. As Ruth also points out:

> You should never underestimate that change is not a top-down process. That any sort of top down driven initiative to change will be taken up in a number of different ways, by the individuals, for a whole range of reasons, that you cannot possibly anticipate.

The change that will emerge from any change programme will be that which has been negotiated by the individuals interacting in that network. So, in managing change from this perspective, we have to make some changes in our assumptions. To reassess what we are attempting to do and the likely outcome of the process.

Revisiting Lewin's change process

By taking this view of organisations and the nature of the networks of individuals that make them up, how would this change the approach to change management? How can we create an environment where individuals can make the choice to change in a way that fits with their personal reality? How we can move the network to the point where the change that emerges moves the organisation to the highest peak of fitness possible? If we return to Lewin's three-stage process of change, we can see how we might approach things differently.

The first stage of Lewin's process is the 'unfreezing' of the organisation, or releasing the organisation from its present stable state to allow change to be made. The conventional view of this is that the change leader should define a vision of the desired future state and convince her followers of the benefits of the new ways of working and the likely downsides of not changing. This is essentially an appeal to the rational self to accept the sense of progress and avoid the consequences of not changing. The story of P&F Ltd clearly shows that there was a need to move the organisation out of its state of denial. To get people to address the need to face a changing market. However, it was not a rational decision to avoid any conversation about the situation but an unconscious reality that meant 'having those conversations about possible change were very difficult'.

The alternative view, that I am suggesting, is to facilitate change by creating an environment where the change emerges from the interaction of those involved in the network, rather than confronting people with a need to change and a prepared rationale for the change, and to engage those involved in the sort of challenging conversations that we have been considering. In this way we can harness the narrative learning of the group as a whole to strengthen the understanding and the interaction between them, thus moving them towards an 'edge of chaos' condition where innovation will prompt change.

Lewin's view of change reflects a time when change could be viewed more easily as a discrete event. In today's world change is, more than ever, a continuous process. Rosabeth Moss-Kanter (1984: 282), Harvard Professor of Business Administration, writing more than 30 years ago, referred to what she termed the pre-history of change. She points to the ongoing nature of change and how the previous experience of change initiatives influences an individual's willingness or ability to change in the present. Any change initiative needs to be managed in the context of all that has gone before. Recognising that the current realities of the individuals involved are based on their past experience and their response to any new change programme will be driven by that. The 'unfreezing' stage then is part of a continuous history of change which needs to deal with that legacy of past experiences.

The starting point of any change programme is then to engage with those who are being asked to change in a process of open, challenging and narrative-based conversations. Ideally there should be an ongoing narrative in the organisation. A structure of forums for discussion of the issues facing an organisation. A recognition of the successes and failures in the present and opportunities to face the challenges of the future.

As leaders or change managers we need to accept that the change that emerges from the process will not be precisely the change that was envisioned at the outset. The new way of working or the new culture will be the one that has emerged from the interaction in the network. It will be the result of a self-organising process that is the sum of all the changing realities of those involved in the process. The change may well approximate to that originally intended. The new computer system is in place or the revised work process may have been introduced but individuals will have negotiated an approach to it that satisfies their individual self-beliefs and unconscious drives. They will have made the choice to change on their own terms and in line with their unconscious reality. As such, leaders should acknowledge that effective and accepted change is a bottom-up, rather than a top-down, process. The role of the change leader is not to direct and control change but to encourage and facilitate the emergence of change. To promote conversations, allow individuals to reform their realities and to capture the outcome in terms of the change to be implemented.

Lewin's second stage is the implementation of the determined change. Again, the conventional view is one of directive action including communicating and reinforcing the future vision, getting rid of obstructions and training and coaching individuals in the new ways.

In our alternative view, we recognise individuality. We accept that how we act in the present and the choices we make about change, is driven by our past experience, our current reality and our expectation of the future. Rational arguments of how better that future will be, if we accept a particular change, will be processed in our conscious brain but that will only be reflected in our choices in the present once our unconscious reality has been reshaped. Once any deeply held and potentially conflicting beliefs have been addressed and reconciled to it.

In the change process, we need to provide opportunities for individuals to confront their realities and to deal with any issues that may prevent them making a choice to change. Change leaders should create opportunities for narrative conversations and the space to challenge assumptions, enabling people to interact and explore their feelings in a way that allows their reality to be made explicit and reformed in order that they can accommodate the change. In this way resistance is accepted in the change process as a natural and essential ingredient, as something to be worked with rather than something that just needs to be dealt with or 'got around'.

Jim's story gives us a powerful example of how the one-to-one interviews and, in particular, the Values and Beliefs sessions prompted the individuals to confront their deeply held feelings about change. In this way, many of those involved were able to make the choice to change. Beyond the explicit objectives of that particular change programme the story illustrates how other changes emerged spontaneously from the interactions in the network. Jim himself went on to a career direction that emerged from his changed reality. The specific operational and performance changes put in place at the outset of the programme were changed and developed by the conversations that were instituted.

Lewin's final stage is the 'freezing or refreezing' of the organisation to secure the change and make it the new way of working. It is generally accepted that any 'permanently cemented' change in an organisation is likely to be overtaken quickly by the next process; however, conventional writing does still talk about institutionalising the change by, for example, highlighting how the change has improved performance. Top managers are expected to personify the new approach and to 'walk the talk'.

Taking an alternative view of change

A complexity perspective places an emphasis on how people act in the present. The choices that we make about change happen in the now. They are influenced by past experience and future expectation but they are a continuous process from which future change emerges. The notion of 'unfreezing and refreezing' the process in a 'one step at a time' sequence does not work in reality. So, change leadership or management is an ongoing, continuous activity. The role of the leader should be to be get the best outcome from the interaction of the networks that make up the organisation by strengthening the connections within them, creating a culture of change by choice where individuals are challenged to influence the thinking and actions of their colleagues and enable effective change.

In taking this view of change we are able to accept and facilitate its emergent nature. The sort of non-linear interactive networks, that organisations are, will be at their most creative and able to produce innovative solutions when they are acting close to the 'edge of chaos'. Where the role of the change manager is to facilitate the emergence of creative change rather than to impose a predetermined solution.

Choices can only be made in the present, in what philosophers from Herbert Mead on have referred to as the living (or specious) present, the point at which the choices we make are driven by a combination of our current perceptions of our past experiences and our expectations of the future, expectations that are continually formed and reformed in our ongoing conversations, or what Stacey (2001) refers to as complex responsive processes, in that living present. We cannot change the facts of the past or know an unknown future. Equally, we cannot change the choices that are made in the living present:

that present is now the past as we constantly move on. What we can do is make the decision to influence the choices we make in the unfolding living present. Our perceptions of the past and expectations of the future are not fixed; they are constantly being reformed in the conversations, conscious and subconscious, vocalised and non-vocalised, that continue in the living present. We can change the processes, improving them through lean design or by creating new ones, but the adoption of those changes and the way in which they are implemented is a choice based on past experience: 'just another management fad!' and future expectation: 'it'll never work!'

Successful change management deals, in the living present, with the negative legacies of individuals' past experiences and creates confidence in a positive outcome to which the business aspires: a virtuous circle of positive reinforcement through a sequence of responsive processes that creates a belief in successful change.

I started this volume by saying that 'I hate change', and that is a common expression that we hear in the resistance to organisational change. We have been paying attention, here, to what is actually going on in organisations, society and evolution, and we see that change is what we are. It is a part of our DNA, as without it we would not be where we are. The alternative view that I have set out here shows that, however much we protest about the prospect of change, it is an essential part of our makeup, and the role of the change manager should be to facilitate the free expression of that natural process.

References

Eagleman, D. 2011. *Incognito: The Secret Lives of the Brain*. Canongate: Edinburgh.
Moss-Kanter, R. 1984. *The Change Masters: Corporate Entrepreneurs at Work*. Unwin Hyman: London.
Stacey, R. D. 2001. *Complex Responsive Processes in Organisations*. Routledge: London.

Index